Heaven Misplaced

HEAVEN MISPLACED

CHRIST'S KINGDOM ON EARTH

DOUGLAS WILSON

canonpress
Moscow, Idaho

Published by Canon Press
P.O. Box 8729, Moscow, ID 83843
800–488–2034 | www.canonpress.com

Douglas Wilson, *Heaven Misplaced: Christ's Kingdom on Earth*
Copyright © 2008 by Douglas Wilson.

Cover photography (Sainte-Chapelle Cathedral, Paris) and author photo by Mark LaMoreaux.
Cover design by David Dalbey.
Interior design by Laura Storm.

Printed in the United States of America.

Library of Congress Cataloging-in-Publication Data

Wilson, Douglas, 1953-
  Heaven misplaced : Christ's kingdom on earth / Douglas Wilson.
    p. cm.
  Includes index.
  ISBN-13: 978-1-59128-083-4 (pbk.)
  ISBN-10: 1-59128-083-5 (pbk.)
  1. Eschatology. 2. Christianity--Forecasting. 3. Christianity--21st century. 4. Church history--21st century. I. Title.

10 11 12 13 14 15   9 8 7 6 5 4 3 2 1

For
LUKE JANKOVIC,
father of faithful generations,
full of hope and love

CONTENTS

INTRODUCTION

This is a book about the future history of our world, about the future and destiny of the human race. Since the future is not something we are permitted to see directly—only God sees the end from the beginning—in order for this book to be anything other than an exercise in conceit, it has to be based squarely on what God has revealed to us in His Word. What has God actually *promised* us? Only God knows the end from the beginning, and while He has not given us every detail about the future, He has in fact revealed a great deal to us.

But unfortunately, what has been given to us has been greatly obscured by discouraging and mistaken assumptions. Most Christians believe in one way or another that the history of our planet is going to go from bad to worse, accelerating as we get near the end. At the same time, all Christians believe that after human history is over, and the day of resurrection is past, our experience will be one glory replaced by a greater glory, one after the other, world without end. No Christian is pessimistic about final glory. But most Christians are pessimistic about the course of history prior to the Second Coming of Christ. In this view, the world is God's Vietnam, and the return of Christ consists of the few lucky ones helicoptered off a roof during

9

the fall of Saigon. When we get out of *here*, then there will be good times—but not before.

The view advanced in this book is almost precisely the reverse. This book is an introduction to historical optimism. This is the view that the gospel will continue to grow and flourish throughout the world, more and more individuals will be converted, the nations will stream to Christ, and the Great Commission will finally be *successfully* completed. The earth will be as full of the knowledge of the Lord as the waters cover the sea. When that happens, generation after generation will love and serve the Lord faithfully. And then the end will come.

But I have already noted that most Christians don't think this way, and so admittedly this is going to be a tough sell. This could quite possibly include many who decide (for various reasons) to read this book. So let's make an arrangement, you and me.

Whenever someone picks up a work of fiction, there is an implied arrangement between the author and the reader, something the author counts on and the reader gives him, and that something is called "the willing suspension of disbelief." Someone can really enjoy *The Lord of the Rings* and agree to temporarily set aside his knowledge that orcs and elves are not exactly real. But once the reader is in story grip, the story comes alive and is made real to him because of that willing suspension of disbelief. Even if the reader does not really "believe in it" after he has closed the book, he still knows the story far better than he would have if he had been saying, "yeah, right" every other page. He knows the story "from within," even if he cannot accept it at the last.

So let's take the example of Tolkien's great work. He was once asked whether he believed that Middle Earth was real. His reply was, "One hopes." Even a work of fiction, if it is compelling enough, can awaken a deep desire for it to have been true. So here is my proposal. There are many Christians who believe that the future of our world (prior to the Second Coming) is bleak indeed. I am asking them to read this little book as though it were a work of fiction. Just for a short while, I am asking for that willing suspension of disbelief. And if that request is granted, then I believe that a striking feature of this kind of historical optimism will become plain. Every Christian can agree on one thing at least. Wouldn't it be glorious if this really *were* true?

For my part, I want to write as though it were a story because it actually concerns the most wonderful story in the world—which, as it turns out is the story *of* the world. And this means that a few things will be different. For example, this story I'm asking you to suspend disbelief about is built on passages that are probably familiar to you. However, there are different ways to understand many of them, so I'm going to suggest a take that may be unfamiliar—you'll see the difference when the story is told that way. So yes, this is a work of theology, and I will be referring to many Scripture passages. But I don't want to assemble a rock pile of proof texts. My goal, corresponding to the request I have made of the reader, will be to try to demonstrate how *lovely* this belief is. This is an exercise, not so much in systematic theology,† but in lyrical theology.† Of course, if it is not true, then it doesn't matter how lovely it is. We have all had some pretty good daydreams. But if it is altogether lovely, then perhaps some might be persuaded to reconsider if it might actually be true. And if that point is reached, it will become possible to build one's Christian life on *the foundation of all encouragement.*

† **systematic theology:** *the attempt to organize Christian doctrine into an articulate pattern.*

† **lyrical theology:** *a term first used by S.T. Kimbrough, Jr. in 1984, to describe theology that is couched in poetry, hymns and songs, and liturgy. It is characterized by rhythm and expressive of emotion and sentiment. (http://theologytoday.ptsem. edu/tt-V63-1-abstracts.htm)*

Do I really believe that, prior to the return of Christ, the earth will be as full of the knowledge of the Lord as the waters cover the sea? Do I really believe that all the nations of men will stream to their Lord and Savior, Jesus Christ? Do I really believe that Jesus Christ is the desire of nations? I really do. And I hope by the time we are done with this short book, the unconvinced reader will at least be able to say, "One hopes."

1.

ON THE MOUNTAIN OF
THE LORD

Wine on the Lees, Well Refined

In his great sermon "The Weight of Glory," C. S. Lewis has an astute observation—he refers to the reality of the coming resurrection in this way: "We cannot mingle with the splendours we see. But all the leaves of the New Testament are rustling with the rumour that it will not always be so. Some day, God willing, we shall get *in*."*

The point here is not to take anything away from the glory of Lewis's observation. But it does need to be said that the pages of the *Old* Testament were rustling with a magnificent expectation also. These prophecies and glimmers and glorious sketches looked forward expectantly to the coming of the Messiah, and not only to the coming of the Messiah, but to everything else that He would bring with Him. We celebrate this every Christmas, but we sometimes don't pay close enough attention to the wording of these inspired rumors and rustlings. In chapter seven of Isaiah, we read this:

> Therefore the Lord himself shall give you a sign: Behold, a virgin shall conceive, and bear a son, and shall call his name Immanuel. (Is. 7:14)

---

*C. S. Lewis, *The Weight of Glory* (Grand Rapids: Eerdmans, 1949), 13.

Two chapters later, continuing the same great theme, the prophet tells us that the Messiah will come from Galilee of the nations.

> The people that walked in darkness have seen a great light: they that dwell in the land of the shadow of death, upon them hath the light shined. (Is. 9:2; cf. Mt. 4:16)

The thing we must realize is that these prophecies concern far more than just the arrival of the baby Jesus. The prophet Isaiah has more on his mind than providing feel-good quotes for our Christmas cards. Here is something he says in the next breath, something that has shown up on numerous Christmas cards. But we need to stop for a moment and reflect *on what he is actually saying.*

> For unto us a child is born, unto us a son is given: and *the government shall be upon his shoulder:* and his name shall be called Wonderful, Counsellor, the mighty God, the everlasting Father, the Prince of Peace. *Of the increase of his government and peace there shall be no end,* upon the throne of David, and upon his kingdom, to order it, and to establish it with judgment and with justice from henceforth even for ever. The zeal of the LORD of hosts will perform this. (Is. 9:6–7)

When the Christ comes, He will be born of a virgin. When He comes, He will be Immanuel—God with us. When He comes, we will call Him the Prince of Peace. Is that all? Is that it? No—the prophet explicitly tells us that the Messiah is going to accomplish a revolution in the government of heaven and earth. This Son that is given to us will take the government upon His shoulder. The results will be gradual, not instantaneous—but persistent and steady. Of the increase of His government and peace there shall be no end. When the Messiah comes, He will assume His rightful place on the throne of David, as He has done, and He is going to establish His kingdom in judgment and justice. That process will begin when the child is born, and the prophecy will be fulfilled completely "henceforth even for ever." If anyone still doubts, remember that the zeal of the Lord of hosts will make sure it happens.

Historical optimism about Christ's kingdom on earth means that we believe—because the child was born two millennia ago—that since that time, the increase of His government and peace has been unceasing. We believe that the government *is* on His shoulder, not that it *should* be. Jesus believed the same thing, because when He sent His disciples out, it was with this truth as the basis for the commission. "*All* authority in heaven and on earth has been given to me" (Mt. 28:18, NIV).

> For he must reign, till he hath put all enemies under his feet. The last enemy that shall be destroyed is death. (1 Cor. 15:25–26)

In the common assumption shared by many Christians, at the Lord's return the *first* enemy to be destroyed is death. But the apostle here says that it is the last enemy to be destroyed. The Lord will rule from heaven, progressively subduing all His enemies through the power of the gospel, brought to the nations by His Church. And then, when it would be easy to believe that it just couldn't get any better, the Lord will come and deliver the kingdom to His Father, and God will be all in all.

But there is something else. What will it be like as His kingdom grows and expands? What will happen to our sin-plagued world as His government and peace increases?

> The wolf also shall dwell with the lamb, and the leopard shall lie down with the kid; and the calf and the young lion and the fatling together; and a little child shall lead them. And the cow and the bear shall feed; their young ones shall lie down together: and the lion shall eat straw like the ox. And the sucking child shall play on the hole of the asp, and the weaned child shall put his hand on the cockatrice' den. They shall not hurt nor destroy in all my holy mountain: for the earth shall be full of the knowledge of the LORD, as the waters cover the sea. And in that day there shall be a root of Jesse,† which shall stand for an ensign of the people; to it shall the Gentiles seek: and his rest shall be glorious. (Is. 11:6–10)

† **root of Jesse:** *At the beginning of this chapter, Isaiah prophesies that "there shall come forth a rod out of the stem of Jesse, and a Branch shall grow out of his roots" (Is. 11:1). This Branch is Jesus, a descendant of King David, whose father was Jesse.*

Now this language is admittedly over the top. It is so over the top that most Christians just relegate it to some time after the Lord comes again. That is the only way they can see that a fulfillment could ever be possible.

But there is a slight problem with this view. The glorious language, the too-good-to-be-true language is in the first half of this passage: predatory beasts become herbivores, and little kids are playing with the cobras. This has to be after the resurrection, right? This has to be after the close of history, doesn't it? No—because verse 10, the one that begins with the words, "And in that day," is quoted by the apostle Paul in Romans 15, justifying his mission to the Gentiles two thousand years ago:

> And again, Esaias saith, There shall be a root of Jesse, and he that shall rise to reign over the Gentiles; in him shall the Gentiles trust. (Rom. 15:12)

The great apostle Paul is appealing to Isaiah as a justification for *his* preaching to the Gentiles. And since then, we have had two thousand years of the Lord's government and peace increasing.

I asked earlier what the characteristics of His rule would be. The passage from Isaiah 11 should take your breath away. The earth will be as full of the knowledge of God as the Pacific Ocean is wet. The root of Jesse will be put up as an emblem, and all the Gentile nations will *stream* to Him. And when they put their trust in Him, they will become people of God and will be taken up to the Lord's holy mountain. What is that mountain like?

> And in this mountain shall the LORD of hosts make unto all people a feast of fat things, a feast of wines on the lees, of fat things full of marrow, of wines on the lees well refined. And he will destroy in this mountain the face of the covering cast over all people, and the veil that is spread over all nations. He will swallow up death in victory; and the Lord GOD will wipe away tears from off all faces; and the rebuke of his people shall he take away from off all the earth: for the LORD hath spoken it. (Is. 25:6–8)

The Lord Himself will make a banquet to end all banquets. The feast will be for all people, and it will be a feast full of marbled beef. The best wine, the aged wine, will be served to all men, and as the banquet is served it will culminate in the destruction of death itself. The Lord will wipe every tear away.

And as we see in Romans, all this happens in the course of history, *not after history is over.* When death is destroyed, as mentioned here, *that* is when the Lord comes. But the coming of the Lord delivers the *coup de grace* to the last, most persistent enemy, death. The growth of the kingdom of God prior to that finale—the establishment of the mountain of the Lord on the earth—has subdued every lesser enemy.

Jesus Christ has ascended to the right hand of God the Father, and in that place He has been given universal rule and authority now. And the Bible says that He will remain seated there until all His enemies are made His footstool.

> The LORD said unto my Lord, "Sit thou at my right hand, *until* I make thine enemies thy footstool." (Ps. 110:1)

The Lord reigns from heaven, exercising all rule and dominion. From that place He will destroy every enemy, and every thought that sets itself up against the knowledge of God (2 Cor. 10:1–5).

The Lord's promises to us are truly staggering, and it is not surprising that we cannot get our minds completely around it. But He delights to give to His people, and one of the greatest gifts that He has given to us *is the future.*

> But as it is written, Eye hath not seen, nor ear heard, neither have entered into the heart of man, the things which God hath prepared for them that love him. (1 Cor. 2:9)

We must fix it in our hearts and minds that these staggering promises do not begin to be fulfilled at the close of history. They *began* to be fulfilled when a child was born, when a Son was given. What is the future of this world, prior to the Lord's coming, going to be like? We can't say, because nothing that good has ever entered into the heart of man. We are slow to believe all that is promised, but the glorious fruition is headed our way nonetheless.

Questions for Discussion
Once the "willing suspension of disbelief" has been granted, this affects the reading of many passages that have a "face value" that is very different than our accustomed reading.

1. Once the Messiah comes, what will His government and peace do? What are the implications of this?
2. When did the apostle Paul locate the beginning of the fulfillment of Isaiah's great prophecy?
3. When the root of Jesse is established as a standard, what will all the Gentile nations do?

2.

HEAVEN MISPLACED

Living in Colonies of Heaven

The first Easter occurred at the time of Passover, which is when the first fruits of the barley crop were presented to the Lord. Pentecost, soon to follow, was when the first fruits of the wheat harvest were presented. As we consider the implications of the resurrection of Jesus, we need to think of it in the right fashion, which means that we have to reflect on the meaning of the first fruits. When we grasp this point, it will transform our understanding of human history. Indeed it will transform our understanding of heaven and earth, and all things between.

> But now is Christ risen from the dead, and become the first-fruits of them that slept. For since by man came death, by man came also the resurrection of the dead. For as in Adam all die, even so in Christ shall all be made alive. But every man in his own order: Christ the firstfruits; afterward they that are Christ's at his coming. Then cometh the end, when he shall have delivered up the kingdom to God, even the Father; when he shall have put down all rule and all authority and power. For he must reign, till he hath put all enemies under his feet. The last enemy that shall be destroyed is death. (1 Cor. 15:20–26)

Christ came back from the grave, and He did so in a glorified, physical body, the same (but transformed) body that had been laid in the tomb. (v. 20). He did this as the firstfruits (v. 20), meaning that His resurrection was one small, tiny part of the general resurrection to come. Adam introduced death *into the world,* and the last Adam introduced resurrection life *into the world* (v. 21). All shall die in this world because of Adam, and so all shall live in this world because of Christ (v. 22).

But we must get the order right—the firstfruits come first, and then the general harvest which occurs at Christ's coming (v. 23). When Christ comes again, the kingdom which He has established (with all rule, authority, and power) will be delivered up to the Father (v. 24). For Christ must reign (at the right hand of the Father) until all His enemies are subdued (v. 25). The last enemy to be subdued in this process will be death (v. 26), after which Christ will come again and render all things back to His Father.

So we need to get this image fixed in our minds and hearts. One of the things we have to resist is a false image of human history, however orthodox we might believe we are on the historicity of Christ's resurrection. This false image works in this way—we think that human history is basically all the same, at least from the Fall to the Second Coming. Things go on pretty much as they have always done. In the middle of this grim history, God placed the cross and resurrection, that resurrection being a completely anomalous event in an otherwise unchanged world. This cross and resurrection are "the gospel," which means we can be "saved," which means in turn that we will go to heaven when we die.

But try this image instead. At the Fall, human history became a movie we are watching in a grainy, scratchy black and white. When Christ rose from the grave, a point of blinding light appeared at that place, and from that place, odd things started to happen—not in the plot lines of the story at first, but rather in the nature of the storytelling itself. Color started to slowly spread out from that resurrection point, and the graininess started to slowly disappear and is gradually transformed into some kind of HDTV. And of course, over time, the story line itself was also affected. We have all seen this kind of thing numerous times. When Aslan breathed on the stone statues and they all began coming back to life in *The Lion, the Witch and the Wardrobe*, that provides the kind of image we should have. When that kind of thing starts to happen, we all look at the screen intently, staring *expectantly*.

So this means that the resurrection was not an odd event in the first century, with all "normal" things staying just the same. The resurrection was the central event of all history, but we have to take this as the central event for all history. It defines history; it establishes the trajectory of the remaining story.

We have missed this, in part, because we have been distracted by a conclusion drawn from our individualistic premises. Because we start with the salvation of "our own stalk of wheat," we find ourselves leaving out the story of the general harvest. But if we started with the harvest, our own stalk would not be left out.

Here is how it works. When we die, before the harvest of all history, what happens to us? We of course go to be with the Lord (2 Cor. 5:8). But over time, this intermediate state, this very temporary state of affairs, somehow became for us our central hope, something we call "going to heaven." We have drifted into a very Greek idea of the immortality of the soul, up in another heavenly dimension somewhere, and we have lost the Hebraic truth of the resurrection of the dead. Instead of physical, we have spiritual, and instead of *here* we have substituted *there*. But this is not the biblical hope.

The Bible doesn't generally speak in our popular way of "going to heaven when we die"—not that it is technically wrong. If we die before the Second Coming, we *will* go to be with the Lord. We *do* go to heaven when we die. The problem is that this interim state has become our overarching paradigm, replacing the biblical hope. The final biblical hope is heaven coming *here*. Thy kingdom *come*, thy will be done, on earth as it is in heaven (Mt. 6:10). Blessed are the meek for they will inherit the *earth* (Mt. 5:5). We look to heaven, not so much because that is where we are going in order to be finally saved, but because that is where our salvation is coming *from* (Phil. 3:20–21).

So the resurrection is not simply a peculiar event in an old and decaying world. It is rather the defining event of the new creation, the new heavens and the new earth. It is harbinger of all things made new. We therefore cannot know the resurrection with an old way of knowing. Resurrection life is *the new ordinary.*

The materialism that came from the Enlightenment was a concerted way to get us back to the old way of knowing, the old way of relating to the authorities, the old way of dying. We are being asked to "know" the world as though Jesus had not been raised in the middle of history. But He has been, and Jesus is now Lord, and Caesar cannot compete with this. This new order been established in the resurrection.

If the dead are not raised, then rulers can rule in the old-fashioned way—"off with his head." That was an argument that (as it seemed for a time) had no proper answer. But the dead are raised, and moreover, the dead *are* raised in the *middle* of human history. The harvest has begun, and the firstfruits have already been presented to God. What could be more unsettling to tyrants? Marx was right about a certain kind of religion—pie-in-the-sky-when-we-die-by-and-by religion *is* an opiate for the masses. But resurrection life and power in the middle of history is a nightmare for the principalities and powers, and their only device is to persuade the churches to stop talking about it. But we believe, and therefore we must speak.

Now this means that if the firstfruits happened two thousand years ago, and the general harvest is sometime in the future, this historical interim is not a time in which "nothing is happening." Rather, to return to Paul's point, it is the time in which we, through the authority of the resurrection gospel, are to be laboring to put down all rule and authority and power, bringing every thought captive.

All this was established in principle in the resurrection (Rom. 1:4), but it was formally inaugurated when Christ ascended into the heavenly places to be received in glory by the Ancient of Days. The Ascension was the glorious coronation of the Lord Jesus. After His resurrection, He established to His disciples that He was in fact alive forever, and then He ascended into the heavens. When He did this, He was received by the Ancient of Days, and was given universal authority over all the nations of men. Earth now has a new capital city—heaven—and we are called to learn how to live in terms of this. And as we learn, we are to teach.

For our conversation [lit., *citizenship*] is in heaven; from whence
also we look for the Saviour, the Lord Jesus Christ: Who shall
change our vile body, that it may be fashioned like unto his
glorious body, according to the working whereby he is able even
to subdue all things unto himself. (Phil. 3:20–21)

As N. T. Wright notes, Caesar Augustus established the Roman col-
ony of Philippi after the battle of Philippi in 42 B.C. and the battle
of Actium in 31 B.C. He did this by settling his veterans there, many
of whom were Roman citizens. This is the backdrop for Paul's com-
ment to the church that was located at this same Philippi. The Roman
citizens of Philippi were there as Roman colonists, intended to extend
the range and force of Roman influence throughout the Mediterra-
nean world. They were not there in order for them to leave Philippi
in order to come back to Rome for retirement.

In this passage, St. Paul is using this striking metaphor for a reason. He says that our citizenship is in heaven (v. 20). We look toward
heaven because that is where Jesus went, which means that heaven
is the place He is going to come *from* when He returns to earth.
The metaphor translated, this means that Jesus was going to come
from "Rome" to "Philippi." He was not going to take "Philippi" to
"Rome." And when the Savior, the Lord Jesus, comes, He is going
to transform our lowly bodies so that they become like His glorious
body (v. 21). What He does in this final transformation is in complete accord with the authority He is exercising now as He brings all
things into subjection to Himself (v. 21). In multiple places, the New
Testament tells us that He is doing this.

If we take this simple metaphor of Paul's at face value, it clears
up a great deal for us. Christians now are living in the colonies of
heaven. Now colonies are not established as feeder towns for the
mother country—just the opposite actually. The mother country
feeds the colonies.

How you take the line of the story matters a great deal. Many
Christians believe the cosmos has an upper and lower story, with
earth as the lower story and heaven as the upper story. You live the
first chapters of your life here. Then you die, and you move upstairs
to live with the nice people—because *only* nice people are allowed

on the second story. There *might* be some kind of sequel after that, but it is all kind of hazy. Maybe we all go live in the attic. But the basic movement in this thinking is from a Philippi "below" to a Rome "above."

But what Paul teaches us here is quite different. We are establishing the colonies of heaven here, now. When we die, we get the privilege of *visiting* the heavenly motherland, which is quite different than moving there permanently. After this brief visit, the Lord will bring us all back *here* for the final and great transformation of the colonists (and the colonies). In short, our time in heaven is the intermediate state. It is *not* the case that our time here is the intermediate state. There is an old folk song that says, "This world is not my home, I'm just passing through." This captures the mistake almost perfectly. But as the saints gather in heaven—which is the *real* intermediate state—the growing question is, "When do we get to go back home?" And so this means that *heaven* is the place that we are just "passing through."

The ideas here—Jesus as Savior, Jesus the Lord, our citizenship, a return that transforms—are all regal and political images. And what this means is that the emperor is coming *here,* and we are the advance team laboring to prepare for that glorious visit.

But though Paul draws on this imagery from certain concepts in the Roman Empire, there are places where the analogy (obviously) breaks down. The pagan emperors did not elevate the people they ruled, but rather just sat on the top of a mountain of peons. But Christ intends to transform our lowly bodies so that they become like His. This means He is promoting us; we are becoming royalty. And the colonies will become as glorious as the motherland.

Representing and establishing royalty on earth has been God's design and purpose from the beginning. One of the indicators of this purpose and intent that is frequently missed is that famous phrase, "image of God." The phrase *image of God* was one in the ancient world that indicated a divinely-imparted royal status. But unlike the pagan use of the phrase, this royalty in Genesis was bestowed on all men and women, and not just a solitary ruler. Through our sin, we succeeded in marring this royal image, but God never relinquished His determination to establish it among us regardless. This is why Jesus came in the way that He did—to restore the image of God in man. This is why Peter can say that we are a royal priesthood (1 Pet. 2:9), and it is also what Paul is talking about in this place. Christ is going to transform our lowly bodies so that they become like His glorious body.

Until we grasp this, we will continue to misplace heaven. Christ is going to come from heaven when He returns. And until He returns, He rules from heaven—which we know on the basis of the Ascension. Consider what was given to Christ when He ascended into the throne room of God. "Sit thou at my right hand, *until* I make thine enemies thy footstool" (Ps. 110:1). "Whom the heaven must receive *until* the times of restitution of all things, which God hath spoken by the mouth of all his holy prophets since the world began" (Acts 3:21). "And there was given him dominion, and glory, and a kingdom, that all people, nations, and languages, should serve him: his dominion is an everlasting dominion, which shall not pass away, and his kingdom that which shall not be destroyed" (Dan. 7:14). And so, knowing this, we wait and work in preparation, patiently, knowing that our labors here are not in vain. In this hope, we take care not to "misplace heaven." The kingdom *comes;* the kingdom does not *go.* So Christ is going to *come* from heaven, and in the meantime, He *rules* from heaven.

Our faith when we consider the Ascension of Christ is the basis for our faith in the coming Descent of Christ. If we stop the story at the Ascension, we are misplacing the point of heaven. If we stop the story when we follow Christ to heaven at the time of *our* deaths, we are misplacing the point of heaven also. Christ has ascended, and this is why the earth is going to be redeemed. And the whole creation is groaning, longing for this to happen. We who have the Spirit long for this as well. One of the purposes of this small book is to teach us how to long for this more intently.

The progression is glorious—from Easter to the Ascension, and from the Ascension to Pentecost. On Pentecost Sunday, we rejoice in the fact that the Comforter has been given, poured out upon us, so that the world might be prepared for the final consummation. This is a central role of the Spirit in the world, and it ties in directly with the purposes of God for this world that we have already addressed.

But if the Spirit of him that raised up Jesus from the dead dwell
in you, he that raised up Christ from the dead shall also quicken
your mortal bodies by his Spirit that dwelleth in you. Therefore,
brethren, we are debtors, not to the flesh, to live after the flesh . . .
For the earnest expectation of the creature waiteth for the mani-
festation of the sons of God. For the creature was made subject
to vanity, not willingly, but by reason of him who hath subjected
[the same] in hope, Because the creature itself also shall be delivered from the bondage of corruption into the glorious liberty
of the children of God. For we know that the whole creation
groaneth and travaileth in pain together until now. And not
only [they], but ourselves also, which have the firstfruits of the
Spirit, even we ourselves groan within ourselves, waiting for
the adoption, [to wit], the redemption of our body . . . Likewise
the Spirit also helpeth our infirmities: for we know not what
we should pray for as we ought: but the Spirit itself maketh intercession for us with groanings which cannot be uttered. And
he that searcheth the hearts knoweth what [is] the mind of the
Spirit, because he maketh intercession for the saints according
to [the will of] God. And we know that all things work together
for good to them that love God, to them who are the called according to [his] purpose. (Rom. 8:11–12, 19–23, 26–28)

The Spirit of resurrection is the Spirit who indwells us (v. 11). Because
our bodies will be raised, we should behave with those bodies now
(v. 12). Those who live for the flesh will die; those who do not will
live (v. 13). Those who are Spirit-led in this way, *these* are sons of God
(v. 14). Our relationship with the Father is intimate and *holy* (v. 15).
This is how the Spirit bears witness, by cleaning up our act (v. 16).
But childhood and adoption cannot be separated from the issues of
inheritance (v. 17). This is an inheritance of *glory* (v. 18).

The whole creation is longing for this moment, looking forward
to it (v. 19). The creation was originally subjected to vanity, but in
hope (v. 20). This is because the creation will be liberated into the
same freedom from corruption that we will have (v. 21). The whole
creation groans in the pains of childbirth (v. 22). Not only does the
creation groan, but we who have the Spirit also groan—with the resurrection in view (v. 23). This groaning is in hope and patient waiting

(vv. 24–25). The Holy Spirit helps us with this task of groaning (v. 26). The Spirit prays for us toward this end (v. 27). And this is what Paul is talking about when he says that all things work together for good (v. 28). This provides us with a straight line to glory (vv. 29–30).

When Adam sinned and fell, the whole creation was subjected to the bondage of corruption. Adam was the lord over the creation, having been given dominion, and as the vicegerent this meant that when he fell the whole thing fell. When the king fell, the kingdom also fell. In the same way, when the second Adam came into the world, it was to do a work of restoration. But the fall was great and the restoration will not be accomplished without much groaning. The groaning here is an image taken from the pains of childbirth, the pains of delivery (v. 22). The created order is pregnant, and at the consummation of all things, will give birth to the new order. This is not something we watch as unaffected bystanders. The creation *groans* this way (v. 22). We—because we have the Spirit—*groan* in a similar way also (v. 23). And the Spirit knows our weakness—He knows that we don't even know what kind of baby it will be. We are like Eve before her first child—imagine what it would have been like to not even know what was happening. And so the Spirit participates in this *groaning* of childbirth (v. 26).

Of course, there are two mistakes to avoid. We are talking about a complete transformation—not a minor refurbishment. One mistake is that of thinking this creation will be burnt to a cinder and not replaced, or replaced by something completely unrelated. The other mistake is that of thinking that this creation will simply be tidied up a bit, with a certain amount of polish and shine. The Lord comes back with some touch-up paint, and regiments of angels scatter around the world to give our Botox treatments.

But we should take a cue from Christ's resurrected body, and our resurrected bodies. These bodies are part of *this* creation, right? And yet they will carry over into the next. Your resurrected body will need something to stand on. The body that goes into the ground is like a kernel of corn (1 Cor. 15:36). There is continuity between the old body and the new, of course, but there is a discontinuity of glory. It is the same with the creation. The whole creation will die, and be gloriously raised. Or, to use another image, the old creation will give birth to the new, and we cannot even begin to fathom how glorious the new will be.

Remember that Jesus was born here too. He is longing to come back as well. But when it first begins to sink in on us that God has not given up on this world, but intends to transform it in glory, certain common questions arise. Didn't Jesus tell His disciples that He was going up into heaven in order to "prepare a place for them"? In my Father's house are many mansions? Yes—the word is *mone,* and the ESV has "rooms." The word denotes temporary lodging, as you would find in a hotel. In this case, it would have to be the nicest resort hotel you ever heard of—a 5,000 star resort hotel.

But doesn't Peter tell us that the elements will melt with a fervent heat, and good riddance (2 Pet. 3:10)? The word for elements is *stoichea,* and is the same word that Paul uses in Galatians for the elemental spiritual forces that had kept them in bondage in the old covenant. When we read *elements,* we tend to think of the periodic table, and not of the spiritual forces that governed the old world. So in my view, Peter is talking about the spiritual government of the world—he compares this event to the flood which had accomplished the same thing (v. 6). But even if the reader doesn't buy it, and wants to take it as referring to the meltdown of the cosmos, Romans 8 requires that this be a transformative meltdown, not an annihilating meltdown. If our body melts down in this conflagration, *our* body will nevertheless be raised.

Because of the Spirit's presence in the world, we have a very great hope. What is the nature of the groaning? What is the Spirit helping us do? The Spirit releases us from our debts to the flesh (v. 12). The Spirit leads us into virtue (v. 13), putting to death the misdeeds of the body. The Spirit stirs us up to pray to our Father (v. 15). The Spirit seals our coming inheritance in glory (v. 17). The Spirit teaches us to groan for better days (vv. 23, 26), and not to interpret the word "better" in our own limited, truncated, and pathetic categories (v. 27). He is the one who searches the deep things of God, and He is the one who knows what is coming. He is the one who groans most eagerly.

Questions for Discussion

Many Christians have confused our final hope of the resurrection with the interim hope that God offers us when we die and go to be Him. This has led to some serious distortions, and it is not too much to say that heaven has been misplaced.

1. When Jesus rose from the dead in the middle of human history, was this simply a very odd event, or did it have ramifications for history itself?
2. When Jesus ascended into heaven and approached the Ancient of Days, what was given to Him?
3. When Jesus poured out the Holy Spirit on the Day of Pentecost, in what three senses has this created a longing, a "groaning," for the day of resurrection?

3.

WHAT ABRAHAM SAW

A City in the Distance

Abraham had a lot less to go on than we do, but he still believed all of this. He rejoiced to see this day. He saw the coming glory.

> Even as Abraham believed God, and it was accounted to him for righteousness. Know ye therefore that they which are of faith, the same are the children of Abraham. And the scripture, foreseeing that God would justify the heathen through faith, preached before the gospel unto Abraham, saying, In thee shall all nations be blessed. So then they which be of faith are blessed with faithful Abraham. For as many as are of the works of the law are under the curse: for it is written, Cursed is every one that continueth not in all things which are written in the book of the law to do them. But that no man is justified by the law in the sight of God, it is evident: for, The just shall live by faith. And the law is not of faith: but, The man that doeth them shall live in them. (Gal. 3:6–12)

Abraham trusted in God, and that was reckoned to him as righteousness (v. 6). And those who do the same thing that Abraham did can rightly be considered his children (v. 7). Scripture prophesied that this would in fact happen to the Gentiles through the gospel declared to Abraham (v. 8). That *gospel* was put this way: through Abraham *all* the nations will be blessed. This bears emphasis. When God preached the gospel, what did He say? He said that all nations would be blessed—that is the gospel. That blessing is identified as the opportunity of being blessed with Abraham (v. 9), and this is for everyone who is "of faith."

So, God told Abraham something, and Abraham believed *God* concerning that something. Note first that the object of Abraham's faith was God. The "carrier" of this, the thing that Abraham wound up believing, was that all nations would be blessed through him.

This is so important. The sentence is *Abraham believed God*, not *Abraham believed in his own way of understanding.* It says that he believed God. The gospel, as it was declared to Abraham, was that the heathen would all be converted. *That* is the gospel. *That* is what Abraham believed. *That* is what Abraham saw. "Your father Abraham rejoiced to see my day: and he saw *it,* and was glad" (Jn. 8:56).

But how do the heathen partake? The contrast is between those who are "of faith" and those who are "of the works of the law." But we must be very careful here. The contrast is not between the grace of "not having to do" and the work of "having to do." This is backwards. The contrast is between the grace of "getting to do" and the condemnation of "not being able to do."

Why are men never justified by the works of the law? It is not because they do them only to discover that they are of no use. The reason law-keeping doesn't work is because men don't actually do it. Those who are of the works of the law are under a curse because— "Cursed is everyone *that continueth not*" (Gal. 3:10). Remember that we are under grace, not under law. Therefore sin is no longer our master (Rom. 6:14).

We inherit the world by faith (together with Abraham) because the just shall live by faith. No man is justified by law. The context of this argument is that no man is justified by keeping the works of law in a Mosaic context. But if we are spiritually wise, we will apply this central biblical principle to *every* form of "law-keeping." Men are summoned to simply believe God, and not to seek to justify themselves through circumcision, Passover-keeping, monkish zeal, or by affirming *sola fide*† in a loud voice.

What do we see if we jump to the end of Galatians 3? What distinguishes these Gentiles who have believed from others who have not (Gal. 3:27–29)? We have to remember two things. First, baptism is the mark of this promise to all nations (replacing the mark of circumcision which was limited to the nation of Israel). True faith was no more visible to the naked eye in the first century than

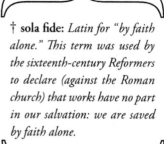

† **sola fide:** *Latin for "by faith alone." This term was used by the sixteenth-century Reformers to declare (against the Roman church) that works have no part in our salvation: we are saved by faith alone.*

it is today. Second, those who are so baptized need to remember the solemn warnings that Paul gave to baptized Gentiles. He commanded them not to make the same mistake the Jews had made—we do not support the root; the root supports us (Rom. 11:19–22).

So we have learned that those who are under the law are under a curse. This is because "being under the law" does not mean that one keeps the law to no avail; rather, it means that one simply does *not* keep it, and is therefore under condemnation. And make no mistake—*all men* have sinned in this way. So, how can sinful men be delivered from this state of condemnation?

> Christ hath redeemed us from the curse of the law, being made a curse for us: for it is written, Cursed is every one that hangeth on a tree: That the blessing of Abraham might come on the Gentiles through Jesus Christ; that we might receive the promise of the Spirit through faith. Brethren, I speak after the manner of men; Though it be but a man's covenant, yet if it be confirmed, no man disannulleth, or addeth thereto. Now to Abraham and his seed were the promises made. He saith not, And to seeds, as of many; but as of one, And to thy seed, which is Christ. And this I say, that the covenant, that was confirmed before of God in Christ, the law, which was four hundred and thirty years after, cannot disannul, that it should make the promise of none effect.

For if the inheritance be of the law, it is no more of promise: but God gave it to Abraham by promise. (Gal. 3:13–18)

We are redeemed from this curse of ours because Christ became a curse in our stead. The Bible pronounces a curse upon everyone hanged on a tree, and Christ was in fact hanged on a tree (v. 13). He did this in order *that the blessing of Abraham* might come upon the Gentiles, that is, the promise of the Spirit through faith (v. 14). Using a human illustration, Paul says that even a covenant made between two men cannot be changed after the fact (v. 15). Now the promise† was made to Abraham and his seed, meaning Christ (v. 16). But the Mosaic law came centuries after this promise was confirmed in Christ (v. 17). The law, which came later, was therefore not the ordained instrument through which the promise was to be fulfilled (v. 18). And remember, that gospel promise was nothing less than blessing for the entire world.

In this passage, Paul is insisting that the promise to Christ in Abraham was foundational, and that the law was added later, for supplementary reasons. The law was therefore an instrument that was subordinate to the promise. The promise was not subordinate to the law.

Now the promise was made to the seed, that is, to Christ, and so the fulfillment of the promise is available to the "seeds" of Abraham, that is, to everyone who has faith in Christ. Paul is not arguing from the law to Christ; he is arguing from Christ to the law. This glorious

† **Genesis 17:3–8:** *And Abram fell on his face: and God talked with him, saying, As for me, behold, my covenant is with thee, and thou shalt be a father of many nations. Neither shall thy name any more be called Abram, but thy name shall be Abraham; for a father of many nations have I made thee. And I will make thee exceeding fruitful, and I will make nations of thee, and kings shall come out of thee. And I will establish my covenant between me and thee and thy seed after thee in their generations for an everlasting covenant, to be a God unto thee, and to thy seed after thee. And I will give unto thee, and to thy seed after thee, the land wherein thou art a stranger, all the land of Canaan, for an everlasting possession; and I will be their God.*

promise is only possible in Christ, and so therefore the seed in Genesis had to be referring to Him.

The promise of blessing for the Gentiles (the sons of Adam) was given to Abraham and to his seed. And yet, all Abraham's natural seed had come under the condemnation of the law through not keeping it. They were so far from bringing blessings to the sons of Adam, that they were actually dragging Adam's disobedience into the line of Abraham. With their Judaic distortions, the life vest became an anvil. This is why the seed of Abraham in the promise *had* to be talking about Christ—otherwise the promise could not be fulfilled at all. Jews and Gentiles, natural sons of Adam, were both under condemnation.

In order to be free, one had to be a child of the promise. But one could not be a child of the promise without also being a child of the great transaction. Christ became a curse for us on the tree, so that in Him we might become the righteousness of God (2 Cor. 5:21). Christ takes our curse, and we take His blessing. We are cursed in Him, and we are blessed in Him. We are crucified in Him, and we are raised in Him.

So not only do we have a contrast between the old Israel and the new, but Paul also gives us a contrast between the old world and the new, between the old heavens and old earth and the new heavens and the new earth. The gospel is the fulfillment of the promise to Abraham, which shows that the gospel is the means by which all the families of the earth will be blessed.

> Howbeit then, when ye knew not God, ye did service unto them which by nature are no gods. But now, after that ye have known God, or rather are known of God, how turn ye again to the weak and beggarly elements, whereunto ye desire again to be in bondage? Ye observe days, and months, and times, and years. I am afraid of you, lest I have bestowed upon you labour in vain. (Gal. 4:8–11)

Back when the Gentiles did not know God, they offered service or obedience to entities which by nature were not true gods (v. 8). But now these Gentiles know God, or rather, Paul says, clarifying himself, are known by God. How is it then that they turn back to bondage? Why do they go back to those weak and beggarly elements (v. 9)? And how is this "turning back" manifested? It is manifested through a zeal for days, months, times, and years—all the various ways of cleaning the outside of the cup (v. 10). Paul is fearful over them, afraid that all his work with them was vanity (v. 11).

The old order of things has passed away. That includes the witness God had established for Himself in that old order, which was the old Israel. In the old order, the Gentiles were in bondage to the elements, and the Jews were in the bondage of having to learn her rudimentary lessons. In that old order, the Jews were the elect people of God, but now that Gentiles have been included in the household of faith in the new world, for those Gentiles to go back to the *godly* old order *was still going back to the old order.*

The Gentile knowledge of God is the result of the grace of God. But if we speak this way too readily, we can come to forget that it is in fact grace. So we remind ourselves that the Gentiles were known by God first, and as a result, they came to know Him.

So faith is one of the great graces in the Christian faith. Abraham, father of all believers, modeled it for us. God told him that the world was going to be transformed through his seed. Abraham simply believed this and God credited it to him as righteousness. Abraham rejoiced to see the day of Christ, and he was glad in it. But Abraham did not just rejoice to see a Christ with no particular job description. He rejoiced to see the Christ who would be the fulfillment of God's promise to him, the promise that Abraham was going to inherit the world. We sometimes think that Abraham's faith was limited to believing that one elderly woman was going to have one son. But the promise went far beyond that. What was that son going to do? What did he represent? He was the appointed instrument, the child of promise, through whom Abraham was going to inherit the world. This was not going to be done through law, but rather through the righteousness of faith (Rom. 4:13). But it certainly is happening and will continue to happen. How could Abraham not inherit the world? God promised.

And so we need to imitate the faith of Abraham. If we are his children by faith, we should really believe the same thing he believed. If we are children of Abraham, we will do the works of Abraham. And the work of Abraham is to believe the One who was sent as the Savior of the entire world.

Questions for Discussion

This chapter and the next two focus on the graces of faith, hope, and love. This chapter concerns the gift of faith.

1. When Abraham believed the promise of God, what was the promise that he believed exactly?
2. If Jesus died in order that the blessing of Abraham might come to the Gentiles, does this mean that God promised Abraham that Christ would come to die as a sacrifice, in order that the promise to Abraham might be fulfilled? Did Abraham understand this?
3. Why does Paul argue that going back to the old, pre-Messiah order was an impossibility?

4.

HOPE INCARNATE

Life Grows in Death

The resurrection of the Lord Jesus was no isolated event. His return from the dead brought with it, in principle, the resurrection of all things from the dead. The power of death, which had held the entire world in thrall, was reversed at that point, two millennia ago, and the power of His new life has since then been working through the world, the way yeast works through a loaf of bread. For this reason, we are children of hope.

> And if Christ be in you, the body is dead because of sin; but the Spirit is life because of righteousness. But if the Spirit of him that raised up Jesus from the dead dwell in you, he that raised up Christ from the dead shall also quicken your mortal bodies by his Spirit that dwelleth in you. (Rom. 8:10–11)

In this passage we find what can only be described as *glorious* argumentation. If Christ is in you, your body will still die (v. 10). As already noted in the second chapter, the Spirit of life that raised Jesus is dwelling in you, and this means you will be raised from the dead by that indwelling power (v. 11). But the resurrection of Jesus was not isolated, and our individual resurrections are not a series of isolated events. Follow his reasoning. If the Spirit of life is in us, we are debtors to Him, and not to the flesh that will die (v. 12). If we are indebted to the fleshly past, we will die. But if we (through the Spirit) mortify the deeds of the body, we will live (v. 13). We are indebted to the future. As many as are led in this way, *these* are children of God (v. 14).

There are two spirits—the spirit of bondage to fear and the Spirit of adoption (v. 15). The Spirit bears witness with our spirit that the resurrection is coming and that we are the adopted children of God (v. 16). But if we are children, we are heirs. If we are heirs, we are joint-heirs with Christ. If we suffer with Him, we will be glorified together in Him (v. 17). *And therefore the sufferings of this world are not even worthy of comparison with the coming glory* (v. 18). And so the creation longs for us to be clearly shown as sons of God (v. 19). The creation was subjected to vanity in hope (v. 20). This creation will be delivered from corruption and will be ushered into our liberty (v. 21). For this reason, the whole creation groans (v. 22). And we Christians, with the first fruits of the Spirit, also groan for the resurrection (v. 23). For we are saved *toward* something (v. 24), and we wait patiently for that day of resurrection (v. 25). Because we are saved toward something, we have hope. And the Spirit helps us in this groaning (v. 26). And Christ knows how to pray because He knows the mind of the Spirit (v. 27). Now, in *this* sense, all things work together for good (v. 28). Those who are foreknown are as good as glorified (vv. 29–30). How should we respond to all this? If God is for us, who can be against us (v. 31)?

There are some staggering things set before us here. But we can miss them by looking to the flesh for guidance. For those who are worldly, for those who do not put to death the misdeeds of the body, all these glory words will be just so much gibberish. But for those of us who embrace these realities by faith, it is necessary to recognize that we still fall short of God's ultimate design, which is why in this instance our understanding is expressed with groaning. The creation groans, we who have the first fruits of the Spirit groan, and the Spirit Himself groans along with us, helping us in our weakness. This means that we live in weakness here on earth and need to be helped. It does not yet appear what we shall be, but the Spirit helps us as we long for it. And when Paul tells us that the Spirit helps us in our weakness, the verb he uses means to "lay hold along with," as though we were carrying a heavy log—we holding one end and the Spirit holding the other. We need help because we don't "get it." But at least we know that there is something we don't get.

Now the resurrection of the dead in Jesus *started in the middle of history.* Our resurrection is connected to His. Jesus was raised from the dead by the power of the Spirit (v. 11). That same Spirit, with the same plans and the same intent, dwells in us also. Christ's resurrection was the first fruits of the new heavens and the new earth, and we have been given the first fruits of the Spirit (v. 23). Now because the Spirit of Christ's resurrection is in us, and because we are in the world, it follows that the Spirit of Christ's resurrection is in the world—and moreover, *the world knows it.* Christ's resurrection power is walking around today, here. And the whole creation longs for what is coming (v. 19). The resurrection of the Christ is cosmic resurrection and redemption (Col. 1:20).

Paul says those who are children of God are heirs of God, and they will inherit all things in Christ (Rom. 8:17). But who are the children of God? Who is indwelt by the Spirit of Christ? Is the Spirit ever in us as some kind of inert substance? No, the Spirit of Christ, who works in us, works in us *actively.* And if the Spirit of Christ is absent, then a man does not belong to Christ (v. 9). So what does this active Spirit do? He dwells in us (v. 11). He gives strength to our mortal bodies (v. 11). He empowers us to put to death the deeds of the body (v. 13). Moreover, He leads us to put to death the deeds of the body (v. 14), and as many as are so led, *these* are sons of God. He impels us to cry out, "Abba, Father!" (v. 15). He bears witness to our spirit that we are children of God (v. 16). He impels us to groan for the resurrection (v. 23). And He is tender with us in our weakness in all these things, helping us (v. 26).

So the apostle Paul wants to help us see our lives in this way. We have two directions in which we may look, and they are as follows. From the vantage point of our present sufferings, we may look back at the old creation, a creation which ends in the death of all living things. We may look to the way of the flesh, but the days of the flesh are numbered. If we look that way, we will die. But from the vantage point of the Spirit's present work, in the midst of our sufferings, the only alternative is to look to the future, but not to the immediate future, the day after tomorrow. We are looking to a world made new, not because we deny this present world, *but rather because we understand what is currently going on in this present world.* All this will be dismissed as "pie in the sky" by scoffers, but we should not be swayed by them. Those who dismiss heavenly pies are not to be trusted with earthly pies.

Our present sufferings, however great, are not worthy to be compared to the glory that is coming for us (v. 18). Now here is the important shift that has to occur in our thinking if we are to grasp this, if we are to grow in the hope of glory as we ought. All Christians believe that the Second Coming is going to be glorious, abrupt, and sudden. Further, many Christians see this event as coming from outside our world entirely, an invasion from supernatural space. But if you read back through this chapter, you should see that the striking thing about the Second Coming is that it will be the culmination of what is happening right here, right now. The new humanity is going to be finally and completely formed and born, but it is *this* world that is pregnant with that glory. The relief will be great, but it will be relief from the travail of *this* world.

In other words, Jesus *will* come out of nowhere from heaven to the world, and He will raise the dead, and we will meet Him in the air on His way down. But what He comes to isn't an unchanged world, but a world transformed by His resurrection. As more and more nations stream to Christ, the power of His resurrection is going to take up residence within individuals and nations both. And so the blessed hope at the end of history is something that is in the works now.

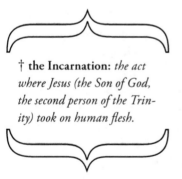

† **the Incarnation:** *the act where Jesus (the Son of God, the second person of the Trinity) took on human flesh.*

We have to come to grips with the fact that when God became man, that one event altered human history forever. Jesus was not born of a virgin in order to conduct "a short visit" of thirty-three years, after which everything returned to normal. The Incarnation† was the beginning of the great transformation. John describes it this way:

> In the beginning was the Word, and the Word was with God, and the Word was God . . . And the Word was made flesh, and dwelt among us, (and we beheld his glory, the glory as of the only begotten of the Father,) full of grace and truth. (Jn. 1:1, 14)

John's gospel begins with the words *in the beginning,* deliberately echoing the first words of Genesis (Gen. 1:1). Just as God had created the heavens and the earth, so in the arrival of Jesus, He was *recreating* the new heavens and the new earth (Jn. 1:1). In the beginning was the Word, and the Word was *with* God, and the Word *was* God. What does this mean? The "withness" is defined by the word *Word.* The Word was *with* God the Father in the way our words are *with* us. They are not the same. And yet, at the same time, our words reveal who we are and are to be identified with us. We are what we speak. Out of the abundance of the heart, a man speaks, and we are this way because God is the same way. Out of the abundance of His heart, He speaks.†

Now, this perfect Word, this Word that came from the Father without any degradation of meaning, this Word which was also to be identified with God—what did He do? He became *flesh,* John says, and dwelt among us (v. 14). Did this degrade the Word? No, John says, "We *beheld* his glory" (v. 14). What glory? The glory of the only begotten of the Father. What glory? A glory that was *full* of grace and truth.

† **Luke 6:45:** *A good man out of the good treasure of his heart bringeth forth that which is good; an evil man out of the evil treasure of his heart bringeth forth that which is evil: for of the abundance of the heart his mouth speaketh.*

In one sense, Jesus said that He was the only one who had seen the Father (Jn. 6:46). But in His famous encounter with Philip later in this gospel, Jesus also said this:

> Have I been so long time with you, and yet hast thou not known me, Philip? he that hath seen me hath seen the Father; and how sayest thou then, Shew us the Father? (Jn. 14:9)

This means that God has spoken Himself into a very imperfect and broken world, and He has done so *perfectly*. What are the implications of this? *This could not happen without bringing the world to life.* Put simply, John 1 tell us that God entered the world as a man, and in John 5 we discover why—to give life (Jn. 5:26).

Jesus is the Savior of the world, and He is, by necessity, Savior of the world. But man in his sinful condition does not want to be saved. That is part of what it means to be a sinner. It means that man tries, by various strategies, to put himself out of God's reach. Some want to do it arrogantly, like the modern atheist who says there is no God. Communication is not possible, and the problem or fault is on God's end: He is to blame for not existing. But others want to pretend to a kind of humility, and so they act as though the problem is with our hearing and not with God's speaking. "Yes," they say, "God speaks perfectly, but we are finite, limited, and selfish. We cannot pretend to know what He has said to us because we can only hear imperfectly. Anyone who claims to have understood what He has said must be really arrogant." This kind of thinking is foolishness. It makes a great show of adjusting to limits, and refuses to consider the implications of the Incarnation. Francis Schaeffer put the answer well in the great title of his book: *He is There and He is Not Silent*. Many recent thinkers believe that anything that proceeds "downstream" from a source is necessarily a degradation. Only the source can be pure.

But their problem is that they have forgotten that God is triune, and that His Word is the *express* image of His person (Heb. 1:3). This is not like a line of Xerox copies, with each one getting progressively blurrier, or some version of the telephone game, where the message gets increasingly garbled. Away with all that! We are *Christians*.

God the Word (*Logos*) is not the *Om* of Eastern mysticism. He does not smudge everything. He *articulates* it; He speaks it. Our Lord encompasses, and embodies, and exhibits *everything* that words do—exclamations, sentences, poems, stories, parables, sermons, lectures, novels, whispered conversations, propositions, questions, and more poetry. God speaks and we are called to *listen*.

Our triune God is not one frozen word, eternally stuck. The conversation is everlasting, glorious, swift, and beyond all reckoning. If this conversation were water, do not think of an infinite static ocean, but rather of an infinite cascading waterfall. No top, no bottom, no sides, no back, no front—and falling with infinite swiftness. God the Father speaks all of it, and the Word is all that is spoken. But who could possibly understand any of this? The Holy Spirit is the Wisdom that understands this infinite conversation, *all* of it.

> But God hath revealed them unto us by his Spirit: for the Spirit searcheth all things, yea, the deep things of God. (1 Cor. 2:10)

Now, consider the nature of the miracle we celebrate at Christmas. Without losing *anything* "in the translation," God brought *His* conversation into *this* world, starting in the womb of a young Jewish woman. The Word (the Word we have been speaking of) became *flesh,* and all carnal philosophy and wisdom are weakened by this Incarnation.

But none of this was done to establish our idols or to keep them from tottering. What God has actually said in this great and stupendous miracle is a threat to all our smarmy "good works"—all the things we would have liked an eternal Word from God to have said and done. But what does this Word *do?* Chats with hookers and drug addicts. Cries out in terrible thirst on a gibbet. Preaches hellfire and promises torture for the obstinate. Forgives the men who flayed Him.

God the Father has not stopped talking. He is still speaking, and Jesus is still that Word. Our God is not a quiet God, who spoke briefly two thousand years ago. That time in history—our Lord's perfect life of obedience, His death on the cross, His resurrection, and His ascension to the right hand of the Father—was the critical chapter in the long story of the world. If we don't understand what was said and done in that chapter, we cannot understand anything else. But if we understand that chapter, we will go forward from it with wisdom about the chapter we are in and the chapters to come. And this is why we are telling the story of the salvation of the world.

We need to understand the drift of this conversation. God spoke Himself into our world, and He did this *in order to save this world.* This means that we cannot spiritualize our salvation. Christ brought it here, which means that we must not try to turn it into an abstract belief. We must not be gnostics†—Christ was born into this world, in a town that is still with us, and which many of us have visited. Christ lived His life in this world. He was crucified here, and in His resurrection He planted this new life in the middle of this dead world and promised His Father it would grow and spread. Spiritualizing it, or relegating all this to heaven in some future age, is a very tragic form of unbelief. Christ did not just rise from the dead and zip back to heaven. He touched people here before He left (1 Jn. 1:1–3), and we must come to understand that His life is contagious. It must spread until the entire world is alive.

† **gnostic:** *someone who despises physical things and favors spiritual things, believing that matter (the stuff our world is made of) is inherently evil and inferior to abstractions (thoughts, beliefs, ideas, philosophies, etc.).*

Questions for Discussion

This chapter, the one before, and the one after all focus on the graces of faith, hope and love. This chapter is about God's gift of hope.

1. Why is it important that the Spirit who raised Jesus from the dead is the same Spirit who indwells all Christians today? What implications for human history come out of this?
2. In what sense is the Second Coming of Christ a discontinuous event? And in what sense does it "top off" what God is already doing?
3. When God spoke His Word into the story of our race, did that Word say anything surprising? Like what?

5.

INEXORABLE LOVE

That the World Through Him Might Be Saved

We tend to veer into one of two errors in our view of future history. Either we plunge into a very exciting study of the "end times" and become consumed with the book of Revelation and newspaper reports about the European Union, killer bees, trouble in the Middle East, and so forth; or we dismiss the whole thing with a wave of the hand and a joke—and it is usually the same joke. "I'm a pan-millennialist. Everything will pan out in the end." But much more is involved in this subject than the particular "chronology" we set for the events at the end of the world. Christians must come to understand that our doctrine of the power of the cross—and the love of God exhibited there—will necessarily be at the heart of our doctrine of the future history of the human race.

> And we have seen and testify that the Father has sent the Son *as Savior of the world.* (1 Jn. 4:14)

The apostle John tells us that he, and others with him, had seen something and they testified to it. Now our duty as Christians is to stand with the apostles, and join our witness to theirs. But how can we do this if we do not see what they saw? And how can we testify to something we have not seen? *They* saw that the Father sent the

Son with a particular purpose in mind—this is the will of the Father to which Christ was submitting in the garden when He prepared to go to the cross. The Father sent the Son *to be the Savior of the world.* The words are very plain, and words very much like them are found throughout all Scripture. This is the witness of the apostles. Is it ours? Have we seen this? If we have not, is it possible that we're just not paying the right sort of attention?

What was the mission of Jesus? Or first, what was *not* the mission? "And if anyone hears My words and does not believe, *I do not judge him;* for I did not come to judge the world but to save the world" (Jn. 12:47). Now Jesus says that He did *not* come to judge the world. But what do most Christians think Jesus is going to do when all is said and done? Right. Judge the world.

We see the same thing in a very famous passage indeed. "For God so loved the world that He gave His only begotten Son, that whoever believes in Him should not perish but have everlasting life. For God did not send His Son into the world to condemn the world, but that the world through Him might be saved" (Jn. 3:16–17). The reason Christ came into the world was to save it—and most emphatically His mission was not to *try* to save it.

The untutored Samaritans in John's gospel knew more about this than many contemporary Christians do. "[A]nd we know that this is indeed the Christ, *the Savior of the world*" (Jn. 4:42). Why did Christ give His flesh on the cross? For the life of the world (Jn. 6:33, 51).

This is the power of propitiation. Now propitiation is the averting or turning aside of wrath. God's wrath was upon our world for its sinfulness and in the cross Christ provided a propitiation for the entire world. "And He Himself is the propitiation for our sins, and not for ours only but also for the whole world" (1 Jn 2:2). Notice that God is attempting nothing—He is, in fact, doing something. "The next day John saw Jesus coming toward him, and said, 'Behold! The Lamb of God *who takes away* the sin of the world!'" (Jn. 1:29). He does not *offer* to take away the sin; He takes it away.

Because of this, we have a ministry of reconciliation. "[T]hat is, that God was in Christ reconciling the world to Himself, not imputing their trespasses to them, and has committed to us the word of reconciliation" (2 Cor. 5:19; cf. Rom. 11:15). We carry on the ministry which was first entrusted to the apostles, and that ministry is to proclaim the word of reconciliation. Now this is *committed* to us, *entrusted* to us. What can be said of unfaithful emissaries who alter the message? We no longer tell people that God actually reconciled the world to Himself, because we don't think that He actually did *that*. We are as full of unbelief at this point as the people we preach to!

There are two popular choices, both bad. Popular evangelicalism wants the atonement† to touch every last man, woman, and child. But in order to get it to do so, the touch is made *ineffectual*. On the other hand, pessimistic Calvinists want the touch to be potent and effectual . . . for a few hundred people. But we are called to preach an effectual cross, an efficacious† cross which will manifest itself among all who hear— and all *will* hear—in nothing less than the salvation of the entire world. This salvation is secured *by faith.* "For the promise that he would be *the heir of the world* was not to Abraham or to his seed through the law, but through the righteousness of faith" (Rom. 4:13).

† **the atonement:** *the act by which our sins are forgiven by God and we are reconciled to Him. Christ's death on the cross made this reconciliation possible.*

† **efficacious:** *to say that the cross is "efficacious" is to say that it actually achieves something.*

Our Lord Jesus Christ "was the true Light which gives light to every man coming into the world" (Jn 1:9). Do we really think so? Do we really believe that? Jesus was crucified in a public way, and so His death must have public ramifications. There is no way to be fully faithful to the message of His death and resurrection in private. Private faith in this public event cannot, in the very nature of the case, remain private. The love of God, as displayed in the cross, is as public as it gets.

> For I determined not to know any thing among you, save Jesus Christ, and him crucified. . . . Howbeit we speak wisdom among them that are perfect: yet not the wisdom of this world, nor of

the princes of this world, that come to nought: But we speak the
wisdom of God in a mystery, even the hidden wisdom, which
God ordained before the world unto our glory: which none of
the princes of this world knew: for had they known it, they
would not have crucified the Lord of glory. (1 Cor. 2:2, 6–8)

In this text, we have many wonderful things stated, and a number
of other (surpassingly glorious) things only hinted at. When St. Paul
came to the Corinthians, he did not come as a showboating preacher-
man saying, "Look at all this knowledge I have" (v. 1). Rather, he
resolved to know nothing among them except Christ and Him crucified, to keep Christ as the center—the source of truth (v. 2). Paul
goes so far as to say that, as *men* would measure it, he was unquali-
fied to teach them (v. 3). He recalled his messages as being the same
way: delivered not with "enticing words of man's wisdom," but with
God's power (v. 4). And this was because he did not want them to
have faith in the wrong thing—in him or in pretty-boy preachers
instead of God's power (v. 5). We *do* speak wisdom, he says, but it
is not the wisdom of this world's princes, who are coming to nothing (v. 6). We speak a hidden wisdom, now revealed (on the cross,
remember), which God ordained before the world *for our glory* (v. 7).
If the princes of this world had known what was up, they would not
have crucified the Lord of glory (v. 8). In doing this, they arranged
for a spectacular blessing for those who love God (v. 9). And what
this consists of is revealed to us by the Spirit (v. 10).

The danger of radical individualism can be clearly seen in this
phrase from verse 2: "not to know any thing among you, save Jesus
Christ, and him crucified." I grew up in a church which thought it
was the responsibility of the church to preach the gospel every Sunday, with an invitation every Sunday. And why? Because that church
assumed that preaching "Christ and Him crucified" was only about
getting souls into heaven and nothing more. And because Paul's
words were taken in a truncated way, this gospel was limited to the
salvation of invisible souls after they depart from this world. This
gospel had little to say about life here on earth.

But note how Paul approaches this. His message is a message that
topples the princes of this world, and everything that previously had

been under their jurisdiction—and this meant the arts, politics, education, scientific investigation, building fences, cooking, and anything else that men might do. Rightly understood, preaching Christ and Him crucified is as broad as the world.

In the history of the Church, three basic theories of the atonement have developed. They have frequently been articulated in opposition to each other, but this is not necessary at all. They all have a scriptural basis, and we have to learn how to see them all together. If we do, instead of opposing them to each other, we will start to see something of what Paul is addressing here. And if we take one view in isolation from the others, we start to drift toward a rejection of what Paul is describing in our passage.

The first view has been emphasized in the Protestant Reformed world. This line of thought has a long pedigree and has culminated in the Protestant view that Christ died as a substitute, taking on Himself the penalty for our sin.* "For Christ also hath once suffered for sins, *the just for the unjust,* that he might bring us to God, being put to death in the flesh, but quickened by the Spirit" (1 Pet. 3:18).

Abelard is associated with the second position—the view that Christ died in order to set an example for us to follow. The idea is that by sacrificing Himself in this way, He provides a pattern of moral influence. We see immediately that this is pitifully inadequate in isolation, but it is in the Bible. "For even hereunto were ye called: because Christ also suffered for us, *leaving us an example,* that ye should follow his steps" (1 Pet. 2:21). Unlike Penal Substitution, Christ didn't *have* to die for *this* reason. But the Bible tells us He *did* in fact do so.

The third is the *Christus Victor* theme. In this view, the death of Jesus is seen as Him triumphing over the devil and his angels. This too is biblical, but again not in isolation.

> And you, being dead in your sins and the uncircumcision of your
> flesh, hath he quickened together with him, having forgiven you

---

*For an extensive history of this view, see Steve Jeffery, Michael Ovey, and Andrew Sach, *Pierced for Our Transgressions: Rediscovering the Glory of Penal Substitution* (Wheaton: Crossway Books, 2007).

all trespasses; blotting out the handwriting of ordinances that was against us, which was contrary to us, and took it out of the way, nailing it to his cross; and having spoiled principalities and powers, he made a shew of them openly, triumphing over them in it. (Col. 2:13–15)

More could be said, but notice that when we see all these together as parts of a whole, instead of as competing theories, we can see that on the cross, Christ was exercising *all* His offices—prophet (Abelardian), priest (Protestant), and king (*Christus Victor*).

And so this brings us to the question of the new humanity and the old princes. There will be more on this in the next chapter, but we have to touch on it now. Jesus was not murdered in private by thugs, only to come back from the dead in secret, with a select band of followers being told to whisper the news to another handful: "Pssst! Pass it on." *No*, He was executed publicly by the *authorities*, and He rose from the dead in such a way as to declare His absolute authority over all the kingdoms of men, and over everything that they contain. We have to learn how to see the cross in these terms, which is what Paul is insisting on in our text.

When we preach Christ and Him crucified, we are preaching the hope and glory of the world. What God has prepared for us who love Him here, *on this earth*, has not begun to enter the heart of man. What is God preparing to pour out over this whole planet? What is He planning to give to us? What is His saving intent for this world? He is going to inundate our sorry and sinful world with the deep things of God. When the earth is finally as full of the knowledge of the Lord as the waters cover the sea, those seas will be *infinitely* deep. In thinking about the greatness of the Great Commission, you do not ever have to worry about overdoing it.

So the crucifixion is powerful, but only because the resurrection enables us to talk about it. And so we testify to the reality of the resurrection of Jesus Christ. He was crucified, died, and was buried. He came back from the dead on the third day, and He did so in accordance with the Scriptures. This we confess, and we confess it gladly. But it is not enough to declare that Jesus is risen; we must also declare the ramifications of this stupendous fact.

And the times of this ignorance God winked at; but now commandeth all men every where to repent: Because he hath appointed a day, in the which he will judge the world in righteousness by that man whom he hath ordained; whereof he hath given assurance unto all men, in that he hath raised him from the dead. (Acts 17:30–31)

Many modern apologists† think of the resurrection as something that needs to be proven. It is challenged by unbelievers, and so we assemble our arguments to show that Jesus did too rise from the dead. This *can* be appropriate in its limited place, but we should never forget that the New Testament treats the resurrection not as something demanding proof, but rather as something that is a proof. Who is Jesus? He was declared, with power, to be the Son of God by His resurrection from the dead (Rom. 1:4). The resurrection is not waiting around to be established; the resurrection *establishes*.

† **an apologist:** *a Christian who seeks to defend the faith and present it as superior to the religions and philosophical systems of the unbelieving world.*

In this passage, the thing that is established by the resurrection is the fact that Jesus Christ will judge the world. He will judge the world, we are assured, because God the Father raised Him from the dead. This is not a judgment of general mayhem and destruction, which (as we saw earlier) Jesus said that He would *not* do. It is a judgment of salvation and righteousness, and His resurrection is how we know that the world will be judged "in righteousness." This is our basis for telling men that it is no longer acceptable to remain in ignorance: God now commands all men everywhere to repent. This command comes in the resurrection, and it is the *nature* of this command that we are now considering.

We must *not* assume that if Jesus is going to judge the world on this basis that we automatically know what His judgment will look like. It is far too glib to say that His resurrection shows that He has a lot of power and that it would certainly take a lot of raw power to judge the world, and so He will judge the world just like anyone else around here would, only bigger and stronger. *No.* The resurrection does not just show that He has the authority to judge (though He most certainly does); it also reveals something to us about the nature of the standard to be used, and the nature of the saving blessing contained within His judgment. The message is *not* "Jesus is coming again, and boy, is He angry."

Who is this judge? He is the resurrected victim of a judicially-rigged murder. Christ is returning, and He is returning with deliverance from the old ways of death disguised as "justice." Prior to that return, He commands His people to declare His standards of justice, His ways of justice, which are completely contrary to the pagan ways of death. We can take comfort in the love of God because the sin we must be delivered from is the sin of confounding the Spirit of God, the *comforter,* with the spirit of Satan, the *accuser.* And that is quite a confusion—one that the resurrection dispels entirely.

Christ is in the process, right now, of overthrowing satanic civilization. The name of Satan means *accuser.* He is the one who delights in pointing the finger at unrighteousness, at the mistakes and failings of others. He is the accuser of the brethren, day and night (Rev. 12:10). He is the one who comes into the presence of God, prepared to accuse Job. The word *devil* renders the word *diabolos,* which means "slanderer, blasphemous accuser." Satan delights in juggling turmoil, stirring up trouble, circulating false reports, encouraging people to cut others absolutely no slack. This is his way. But this is done to a purpose; it is not just mischievous and impish behavior.

Pagan civilizations have always been built on the bedrock of scapegoating murder—this kind of turmoil is managed until it gets to a crisis point, and then everyone wheels on the designated victim. After the murder of this victim, everything becomes tranquil again. These kinds of sacrificial and ritual murders used to work. From Oedipus at Thebes, to Remus at Rome, to Julius Caesar in Rome, we see this happen over and over. For the carnal man, this is the most natural thing in the world. Accusation equals guilt, and condemnation for him equals salvation for us. This is satanic—but do not confuse this satanism (as biblically defined) with things ghoulish. This kind of satanism is most respectable.

But from beginning to end, the Scriptures stand squarely against this pagan mentality—the mentality that is always serene and self-confident about the guilt of the designated victim. Consistently, from Genesis through to the end of the Bible, the Scriptures tell this same story from the vantage point of the innocent victim. This mechanism that is found in all pagan societies is also found throughout Scripture—the difference is that Scripture consistently tells the story from the other side. Think of Joseph sold into slavery by his brothers, falsely accused. Think of Job, falsely accused by Satan in the heavenly courts and by his so-called comforters here on earth. Think of all the prophets, from Abel to Zechariah, son of Berechiah.

And think of the Psalmist. In Stalinist show trials (which were essentially pagan), part of the drill was to get the accused to accuse himself as well, as a vindication of "the system." See, the system works! But the Psalmist, frequently the designated victim of an approaching lynch mob, is about as uncooperative as a victim can get. And we see here a deep irony in the problems that many modern Christians have with the imprecatory psalms† and psalms of protested innocence. We think the language is over the top. The man is sitting on the back of a horse, hands tied behind his back, and a rope around his neck. He looks at the bulls of Bashan round about and calls them a brood of snakes. "*Tsk,*" we think. "That kind of language is a little inappropriate."

† **imprecatory psalms:** *the psalms which cry out for God to punish the wicked, often in language that is neither nice nor polite.*

Another important detail we can see in the Scriptures is the fact that the divide is not between prince and peon, but rather between accuser and accused. Sometimes the accuser is a slave girl (think of Peter), and sometimes the accuser is a prince of the people (think of Caiaphas). Sometimes the accused is entirely defenseless (think of John the Baptist) and sometimes he is the king (think of David). The issue is biblical justice versus worldly justice, always.

Wicked accusers have bad consciences. There is a reason that Herod assumed that Jesus was John the Baptist come back to life. And because of this, the resurrection of Jesus was the ultimate bad news for the "respectability of human justice." The resurrection of Jesus was the death of false accusation; it was the death of carnal civilization; it was the death of death. In the resurrection, Jesus finally and completely crushed the head of the lying, enticing, accusing serpent. The resurrection of Jesus is therefore for our justification† (Rom. 4:25). This is not condemnation—it is only condemnation for those who cling to the old satanic order, which is teetering.

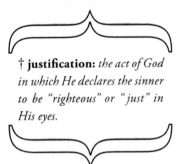

† **justification:** *the act of God in which He declares the sinner to be "righteous" or "just" in His eyes.*

Now because Christ is raised, we are enabled to walk in the power of His resurrection (Rom. 6:8). "He that saith he is in the light, and hateth his brother, is in darkness even until now. He that loveth his brother abideth in the light, and there is none occasion of stumbling [scandal] in him" (1 Jn. 2:9–10). The cross is a scandal to worldly justice because worldly justice is a scandal to the ways of God. Therefore, we are called to love one another.

The death of Jesus was an act of love, as all evangelicals confess. But we must come to a larger view—it was an act of love for the entire world and all that it contains. It was not just an act of love for a select few.

He came to make His blessings flow, far as the curse is found. And that is pretty far—in our legislative halls, in our courts of justice, in our streets. Jesus the Crucified One did not come in order to judge the world, but that the world might be saved.

Questions for Discussion

This chapter, and the previous two, focus on the graces of faith, hope, and love. This chapter is about the love that God has shown to our rebellious world in the cross of Christ.

1. What is the relationship between God's love for the world and His intent to save the world? Will His love result in a saved world, or a world that He tried to save but couldn't?
2. Why is it important that Christ was crucified in public, by the authorities?
3. What are the three views of the nature of Christ's atonement? Are these view mutually exclusive? Why or why not?

6.

THE STRONG MAN BOUND

No Substitute for Victory

Far too many Christians take a phrase from Luther without the faith of Luther. They believe that this world is "with devils filled," but have no knowledge of the "one little word" which fells the evil one. That one little word is *cross*. Christ is the Savior of the world, not only because He died for the world and for lost humanity, but because in His death He overthrew the reigning principalities and powers who had previously ruled. The death, burial, and resurrection of Jesus constituted a revolution in the spiritual government of our world. Tragically, many Christians believe that spiritual warfare is conducted as though Christ never died, or as though His death is historically irrelevant. But this is not what the Bible teaches.

> Now is the judgment of this world; *now the ruler of this world will be cast out.* And I, if I am lifted up from the earth, will draw all peoples [or, all people] to Myself. This He said, signifying by what death He would die. (Jn. 12:31–33)

What had the old world been like? Throughout the Old Testament we see a celestial and angelic government over the nations of men, for the gods of the various peoples were closely identified with their nations. For example, angelic beings stood behind the nations of Persia (Dan. 10:13) and Tyre (Ezek. 28:11–16). General statements are made in which God is contrasted with these beings, and though they are called gods, the Creator God is regarded in another category entirely.

> Among the gods there is none like You, O Lord; nor are there any works like Your works. (Ps. 86:8)

God was sovereign† over such celestials then, but He exercised His sovereignty over and *through* them. They were, in some significant sense, mediatorial princes. But in the Christian age, God has thrown them down and established just one Prince, and He (that Prince) is one of us, a *man*.

† **sovereign:** *having the complete and supreme power that belongs to a king.*

This is why the Christian age is the age in which man comes to maturity. The period of the New Testament is the time of transition between the reign of the celestial princes and the dominion of man in Christ.

> For He has not put the world to come, of which we speak, in subjection to angels. But one testified in a certain place, saying: "What is man that You are mindful of him . . . ?" For in that He put all in subjection under him, He left nothing that is not put under him. But now we do not yet see all things put under him. But we see Jesus, who was made a little lower than the angels, for the suffering of death crowned with glory and honor, that He, by the grace of God, might taste death for everyone. (Heb. 2:5–6, 8–9)

The author of Hebrews did not yet see the promise made to mankind fulfilled. Nevertheless, he does see the fulfillment of this as accomplished and centered *in Christ*.

Now an important distinction is necessary. God, by definition, has always exercised sovereign control over all the world and over every detail in it. The hair on every head has *always* been numbered. But in the accomplished mission of Christ, the cross and resurrection, God established a new *mediatorial* rule in the world. Christ as the eternal Word of God has always been sovereign. But in the events of the Incarnation through the Ascension, God has established His Son as a new mediatorial Prince, replacing the principalities and powers (whether good, bad, or indifferent), and those who trust in Him are now seated and enthroned with Him in the heavenly places.

So we must remember the power of the conquering cross. This is how the New Testament describes it over and over again. If we miss this, we are missing a central part of the impact of the gospel. Note especially the italics in this Scripture:

> However, we speak wisdom among those who are mature, yet not the wisdom of this age, nor of the rulers of this age, *who are coming to nothing.* But we speak the wisdom of God in a mystery, the hidden wisdom which God ordained before the ages *for our glory,* which none of the rulers of this age knew; for had they known, they would not have crucified the Lord of glory. But as it is written: "Eye has not seen, nor ear heard, nor have entered into the heart of man the things which God has prepared for those who love Him." (1 Cor. 2:6–9)

What did these rulers *not know?* They did not know the cross would topple them, and glorify the saints. Jesus said of their ruler, "the ruler of this world *is judged"* (Jn. 16:11). Paul exults in this conquest: "Having disarmed principalities and powers, He made a public spectacle of them, triumphing over them in it" (Col. 2:15). A triumph was a Roman custom, a parade for the victorious general which included a public humiliation of the defeated, shackled and marching in the parade.

So what was the point of the cross? "[T]hat through death He might *destroy* him who had the power of death, that is, the devil" (Heb. 2:14). What Satan offered Christ in the temptation in the wilderness, Christ refused. But Christ did not refuse the offer because He didn't want what was offered. He didn't want it on those terms, but the reason He had come down to earth was to obtain those very kingdoms. He refused the tempter's offer because He was planning to knock him down and take the kingdoms of men from him. "No one can enter a strong man's house and plunder his goods, unless he first binds the strong man. *And then he will plunder his house*" (Mk. 3:27). This is a central part of the message of the New Testament—Jesus took the devil's stuff.

This is why we declare that Jesus is the ruler of the kings of the earth now. Jesus is the God of this world, the God of this age— "Jesus Christ, the faithful witness, the firstborn from the dead, *and the ruler over the kings* of the earth" (Rev. 1:5–6; cf. 11:15; Heb. 6:5). We cannot faithfully declare His cross without declaring what it actually accomplished. What it accomplished was the shaking of the old and the establishment of the new. When this happened, Satan was the god of that age (2 Cor. 4:4), which is not the same as saying he is the god of every age.

There are many places in the Old Testament where the prophets speak of the great renewal of the Church, and of the judgment of God on unfaithful Judaism surrounding the New Covenant. There are many places where the Bible describes the coming dissolution of the Older Covenant order.

> "Yet now be strong, Zerubbabel," says the LORD; "and be strong, Joshua, son of Jehozadak, the high priest; and be strong, all you people of the land," says the LORD, "and work; for I am with you," says the LORD of hosts. "According to the word that I covenanted with you when you came out of Egypt, so My Spirit remains among you; do not fear!" For thus says the LORD of hosts: "Once more (it is a little while) I will shake heaven and earth, the sea and dry land; and I will shake all nations, and they shall come to the Desire of All Nations, and I will fill this temple with glory," says the LORD of hosts. "The silver is Mine, and the gold is Mine," says the LORD of hosts. "The glory of this latter temple shall be greater than the former," says the LORD of hosts. "And in this place I will give peace," says the LORD of hosts. (Hag. 2:4–9)

Consider how the author of Hebrews interprets this "shaking."

> See that you do not refuse Him who speaks. For if they did not escape who refused Him who spoke on earth, much more shall we not escape if we turn away from Him who speaks from

heaven, whose voice then shook the earth; but now He has promised, saying, "Yet once more I shake not only the earth, but also heaven." Now this, "Yet once more," indicates the removal of those things that are being shaken, as of things that are made, that the things which cannot be shaken may remain. Therefore, since we are receiving a kingdom which cannot be shaken, let us have grace, by which we may serve God acceptably with reverence and godly fear. For our God is a consuming fire. (Heb. 12:25–29)

The author of Hebrews is plainly teaching his readers that the shaking of heaven and earth is the removal of the old order of principalities and powers, which includes the old Judaic order, so that the kingdom of God can be firmly established throughout the earth.

The New Testament writers were living at the great transition point. They knew that the old order was coming to an end, and that the new order was being established. As Paul put it, the "fashion of this world passeth away" (1 Cor. 7:31). God broke the old mold, and in Christ He has initiated the pattern of the new. This new pattern or mold is what we are charged to grow up into.

There are other passages as well. The prophet Hosea refers to the coming time of great chastisement.

The days of punishment have come; the days of recompense have come. Israel knows! The prophet is a fool, the spiritual man is insane, because of the greatness of your iniquity and great enmity. (Hos. 9:7)

Why do we not take this as just another general prophecy of judgment? Why do we have to apply it to changing of the ages in the first century? We know because of the words of Christ.

For these are the days of vengeance, that all things which are written may be fulfilled. (Lk. 21:22)

And when Christ spoke this way, He was telling us that it was going to occur within one generation:

Verily I say unto you, This generation shall not pass, till all these things be fulfilled. (Mt. 24:34)

Questions for Discussion

When Christ died on the cross, He was not being defeated. Appearance to the contrary, He was engaged in conquering the principalities and powers.

1. What is the difference between God's sovereign rule over every period of human history, and His rule over the nations now through Christ?
2. What impact did the death of Jesus have on the spiritual rulers of this world?
3. After Jesus bound the "strong man" what did He do? What light does this shed on Christ refusing the devil's offer of all the kingdoms of the world during the temptation in the wilderness?

7.

WHAT THE ANGELS SAID
Goodwill Toward Men

This vision of historical optimism† is not all that common in the Christian world, and so it can get pretty lonely sometimes. But fortunately, once a year the entire nation appears to come around to our way of thinking. You might be shopping in Target for some last minute stocking stuffers and not be at all surprised to hear the loudspeakers reminding you that "He comes to make His

† **historical optimism:** *the conviction that history will end in glorious victory and not catastrophe.*

blessings flow, far as the curse is found." Think of this book as a small effort to get Christians to believe their Christmas carols year-round.

We have trouble with this because Christmas is about grace, and *grace* is one of the most difficult things in the world for sinners to grasp. And as soon as we realize that it is difficult, we turn the "grasping of it" into a contest, giving those with the "right answer" a "best in show" award. But grace doesn't follow our rules. Grace means that some who have the wrong answers will be saved and others who have the right answers won't be.

And there were in the same country shepherds abiding in the
field, keeping watch over their flock by night. And, lo, the angel
of the Lord came upon them, and the glory of the Lord shone
round about them: and they were sore afraid. And the angel said
unto them, Fear not: for, behold, I bring you good tidings of
great joy, which shall be to all people. For unto you is born this
day in the city of David a Saviour, which is Christ the Lord. And
this shall be a sign unto you; Ye shall find the babe wrapped in
swaddling clothes, lying in a manger. And suddenly there was
with the angel a multitude of the heavenly host praising God,
and saying, Glory to God in the highest, and on earth peace,
good will toward men. (Lk. 2:8–14)

As we have all heard many times, there were shepherds in that area,
watching their flocks by night (v. 8). But do not picture a quaint
pastoral scene—this group was much more likely to be a group of
tattooed roughnecks than anything else. Shepherds were not part of
the upper strata of Israelite society. One angel appeared to them, and
the glory of the Lord shone all around them, and they were terrified
(v. 9). The chances are good that the angel interrupted them in the
middle of a ribald joke. The angel told them *not* to be afraid—he
brought them *good* news, tidings of *great* joy, and the message was
for *all people* (v. 10). The basis for the joy was the fact that Christ the
Lord had been born in Bethlehem that day (v. 11). A sign was given—
the baby would be wrapped up, and lying in a manger (v. 12). After
the angel of the Lord had finished, this great message of *peace* was
reinforced by a heavenly *army* (v. 13). The multitude (many thousands) said this (v. 13) in their praise of God:

1. Glory to God in the highest
2. Peace on earth
3. Goodwill toward men

The difference between the Authorized Version and some other
translations is a manuscript issue, not a translation debate, and for
reasons that will become obvious soon, we will be continuing to
follow the AV here.

We have trouble with something as straightforward as "goodwill toward men." We are afraid of grace getting carried away, and so we want to slap some conditions on it. This shows up in some of the other readings. "Glory to God in the highest, and on earth peace among men with whom He is pleased" (Lk. 2:14, NASB). This is consistent with the view that peace is limited to about twenty-eight people—surely God cannot be pleased with any more than that. The goodwill and the peace are dispensed with a teaspoon within a select club, and we no longer have to worry about His apparent spendthrift ways.

But there are too many passages which make God's saving and gracious intention *for the entire world* clear and plain. So we simply ignore them or move them to some otherworldly and heavenly place so that they don't apply to us right here, right now. But we have to do something about the verses that frequently show up on Christmas cards. Surely this doesn't "really mean" that God's goodwill is extended to all men *generally?* Yes, it does. First, quite apart from the manuscript issue, notice what the angel of the Lord had said before the whole heavenly army appeared and sang the chorus. He had said that this was "good tidings of great joy" and it was for "all people" (v. 10).

Now grace spreads in a particular way. The fact that God has every intention of saving the entire world is a gracious message. And those who are worried about us getting carried away with talk of indiscriminate grace don't need to worry. Herod was not a messenger of this grace (although he was an unwitting instrument of it). False teachers are not messengers of this grace (although they too are encompassed by God's purposes). Grace has a backbone and knows how to define itself. Grace is not the word that we are to use as the "open, sesame" of the Church. Grace is not something we do. Grace is not something we can *control.* Grace is not something that we can manage. And this means that we in the Church need to recognize that the guardians of grace are frequently its most dangerous enemies. Grace is God's declared intention of favor for the whole world, whether we like it or not.

The word used here for *goodwill* is similar to God's expressions of pleasure that He pronounced over His Son. "This is my beloved Son, in whom I am *well pleased*" (Mt. 3:17). We are clearly not in this position of favor through any great moral achievement of ours—in the city of David was born a *Savior*. The Savior brought deliverance and forgiveness, which we in our sin desperately needed. We declare this, we preach it, we announce it, which is God's way of spreading this good news. And if God said to all mankind on that first Christmas night, "I don't care how rotten you have been . . . here, in the city of David, a Savior is born," how much more willing would He be willing to say this to *you?* "I don't care how rotten you've been. Got that? *I don't care.*"

We know our Bibles well enough to know that grace, properly understood, does not lead to a life of moral outrage. "What shall we say then? Shall we continue in sin, that grace may abound?" (Rom. 6:1). Of course not. We know the Scriptures in this, but I am afraid that we do not know our own hearts. God's grace is a tsunami that will carry us away and deposit us in places we would not have anticipated—and all of it good. We analyze this carefully and say that we want our grace to be true and pure water, just like the tsunami, but we want it to be a placid pond on a summer day that we can inch across gingerly, always keeping one pointed toe on what we think is the sure bottom of our own do-gooding morality. As the old blues song has it, everyone wants to go to heaven, but nobody wants to die. Everyone wants to cross the Jordan, but nobody wants to get wet.

But we need to get back to the shepherds. God has declared, through His angelic emissaries, His *goodwill* toward our world. He has declared His intentions for *peace.* He did not do this so we would then drastically restrict the message to a tiny "club for peace and goodwill." The gospel is for the *world.* The reason we have trouble with this is that we think it means having the world fit into our tiny club. But it wouldn't fit, and it doesn't want to come. That won't fix anything. So God took decisive action, and through His angels He made a very one-sided declaration to some shepherds.

And so the evening and the morning were the eighth day. We should not be surprised at the pattern of darkness and then light, a pattern which we see not only in the creation of the world, but also in the re-creation of all things.

> I Jesus have sent mine angel to testify unto you these things in the churches. I am the root and the offspring of David, and the bright and morning star. (Rev. 22:16)

A number of these events of the first Christmas occurred at night. The angels announced the good news to the shepherds as they watched their flocks by *night* (Lk. 2:8). The wise men followed the star to Jerusalem and then to Bethlehem, which meant that they were observing it at night (Mt. 2:9). Joseph fled to Egypt with Mary and Jesus, and he did so at night (Mt. 2:14). And one of the most obvious things about Christmas, when we step back and look at it, is that the first Christmas happened in the world's dark night. Evening, then morning, the eighth day. It is not for nothing that our Christmas carols have picked up on this theme—"it came upon a midnight clear," "wake, awake, for night is flying," "how lovely shines the morning star," "as the Light of light descendeth from the realms of endless day, that the pow'rs of hell may vanish as the darkness clears away," "amid the cold of winter when half-spent was the night," and "disperse the gloomy clouds of night, and death's dark shadows put to flight."

But when the sun rises, it does not happen the way a light comes on in a room when you flip the switch. The sun rises slowly. At first, you don't know that anything has happened. It may be just as dark as it was a moment ago, but maybe not. And some time later, you notice that the eastern sky is not what it was. There is *some* kind of light there. The stars that were visible all night begin to disappear. Soon there is just one left—the morning star, the planet Venus, the last indication that day is coming. The next event is for the sun to actually rise, for the day to come. Christ was born at night, and His birth was the arrival of the morning star.

Note John's language again. Christ is the root and offspring of David, and He is the morning star. He is the one who was born at night, and His birth was the arrival of the morning star. It is important for us to allow Scripture to tell us what time it is. If you did not already know, you could not tell the difference between a pre-dawn darkness and a twilight gloaming. Is the sun going down or coming up? The Bible tells us.

Christ Himself is the Word of God, and yet Christians can hold the Word of God in their hands and read it. Christ Himself is the day star, the morning star, and yet Peter tells us that to take heed to Scripture is to have the day star arise in our hearts.

> We have also a more sure word of prophecy; whereunto ye do well that ye take heed, as unto a light that shineth in a dark place, until the day dawn, and the day star arise in your hearts: Knowing this first, that no prophecy of the scripture is of any private interpretation. For the prophecy came not in old time by the will of man: but holy men of God spake as they were moved by the Holy Ghost. (2 Pet. 1:19–21)

Jesus Christ is the light of the world. In the heart of every converted person, He is the light within, the day star in the heart. But whether men are converted or not, blind or not, He is the day star of the *world*, the rising sun of the entire world.

> In him was life; and *the life was the light of men.* And *the light shineth in darkness;* and *the darkness comprehended [overcame] it not.* There was a man sent from God, whose name was John. The same came for a witness, to bear witness of the Light, that all men through him might believe. He was not that Light, but was sent to bear witness of that Light. That was *the true Light, which lighteth every man that cometh into the world.* (Jn. 1:4–9)

We ought not to think that when men are converted, they each become a little lamp, and if enough of them get converted, they will be able to form a consortium and pool their lamps to try to make a sun. The vision of the coming noontime glory does not depend at all on *us* trying to get some momentum up. The sun has risen, and it will continue to do what rising suns do.

Of course, individual response is important, but it is equally important to note what we are responding to. The sun has risen. Christ has come. He is the king. The light covers the world. A return to heathen midnight is an impossibility. Those who walk in darkness now are doing so in a world suffused with light. This is hard to do—you have to remain blind or hide in root cellars. There are ways to stay out of the sunlight, but they are difficult to accomplish. Not only so, but as the day passes, they will get *increasingly* difficult.

> Again, a new commandment I write unto you, which thing is true in him and in you: *because the darkness is past, and the true light now shineth.* He that saith he is in the light, and hateth his brother, is in darkness even until now. He that loveth his brother abideth in the light, and there is none occasion of stumbling in him. But he that hateth his brother is in darkness, and walketh in darkness, and knoweth not whither he goeth, because that darkness hath blinded his eyes. (1 Jn. 2:8–11)

The task of evangelism, now that Christ has risen, is not so much to run around at night, poking our flashlights into corners and cellars. Rather, the task of evangelism is more like pulling back the curtains. "But all things that are reproved are made manifest by the light: for whatsoever doth make manifest is light. Wherefore he saith, Awake thou that sleepest, and arise from the dead, *and Christ shall give thee light*" (Eph. 5:13–14). Get out of that bed! Christ will shine on you!

This is why secularists don't like the first Christmas, and they really don't like the subsequent ones either. What are they going to do? Pass a law? This would be worse than King Canute's acted out parable when he commanded the tide not to come in—this would be Congress passing a law commanding the sun not to shine on places where the First Amendment was in effect.

The good news of "sunrise" does not mean there is no such thing as spiritual darkness, or a final judgment on that darkness. But it does mean that the light overcomes the darkness (Jn. 1:5). Such laws, such foolish resistance, *can* cause some short-term troubles. Think again of Herod and the little boys he slaughtered. But think also about how ineffectual it was. Did he stop the morning star from rising? Did he stop the day from coming? In the same way, we must know that the message of Christmas is not that we have to persuade anybody of anything. The message is far more good news declaration than it is argumentation.

Questions for Discussion

All the gospel points in the direction of the world's salvation. But for some reason, more people are prepared to hear about it at Christmas. Perhaps we can begin there and work our way out to some of the other holidays.

1. To whom was the Christmas message first announced? What significance does this have?
2. When Christ came was He the morning star or the evening star? A rising sun or a setting sun? What difference does it make?
3. If evangelism consists of bringing light to non-believers, what methods do we usually use in attempting this? What methods might be more effective?

8.

AT THE NAME OF JESUS

Every Tongue Confesses

The ascension of Jesus Christ is the coronation of Jesus Christ. This is the point where God formally bestows upon Him all authority in heaven and on earth.

> Wherefore God also hath highly exalted him, and given him a name which is above every name: that at the name of Jesus every knee should bow, of things in heaven, and things in earth, and things under the earth; and that every tongue should confess that Jesus Christ is Lord, to the glory of God the Father. (Phil. 2:9–11)

In the verses just prior to this text, we see the humility of our Lord Jesus Christ. He humbled Himself. He did not grasp at His equality with God. He took the form of a servant. And therefore, God has exalted Him. We see here the ultimate incarnation of our Lord's teaching—the first will be last and the last first. We see that the one who humbles himself is really exalted. There was no greater humbling ever. There will be no greater exaltation ever. And this is where our text begins.

God has *highly* exalted Jesus Christ (v. 9). No higher promotion is possible, for Jesus has been given a name that is above every name.

Not only is this the case, but it is not to be considered as some kind of invisible spiritual truth. Every other name under Jesus is called upon to acknowledge this—every knee must bow, whether in heaven, on earth, or under the earth (v. 10). No place, no location, is excluded. Further, every tongue is under the obligation to confess the Lordship of Jesus Christ, with the glory going to God the Father (v. 11).

The Lord Jesus is of course our example, given so that we should walk in His steps. And this attitude of humility is the fundamental challenge set before us. When Jesus tells us to go to the back of the line, He is actually teaching us how God wants us to go to the head of the line. When Jesus talks about the chief seats in the synagogues, or the seats of honor at banquets, He is not telling us in some revolutionary way to rip those seats out. He teaches us how to get into them. You would think this teaching is so abundantly clear that everyone would get it. We'd all seek the lowest place and as a result all end up in the highest place, with no distinction in honor whatsoever since we'd all humbled ourselves equally. (This complete equality in status and honor is what some would call an egalitarian paradise.) But the power of confused thinking (and resultant disobedience) should never be underestimated.

We disobey the Lord's example in two ways. The first is the error of the permanent pietist—one whose faith rests in his own desire to be holy. He takes the lowest seat, and refuses to budge when invited up. He is too holy to receive God's promotion. He is, in fact, like all pietists, holier than Jesus. The second error is that of the social climber who, despite Christ's pointed warnings, strives directly for the highest seat. But it was well-said by Bonhoeffer that when Christ calls a man, He bids him come and die. This is what our baptism means. Do you not know, Paul argues in Romans 6, that we have been baptized into Christ's death?

Godly authority can only be entrusted to sinners who have died. Without that death, everything touched is abused, whether it is the refusal to exercise dominion (which is *escapist* religion) or the abuse of dominion (which is *despotic* religion). So Christian preachers have (at least) two important duties to discharge. One is to preach the gospel (*euangelizo*), the good news, telling sinners that they must repent and believe, calling upon the Lord for salvation. The other duty is represented by the Greek verb *kerusso,* which has the sense of heralding or announcing. In this sense, the duty of the Christian preacher is to announce to the world the One who is the new Prince, the One who is established as the King.

Scripture teaches that God has given Jesus the name that is above every name. This is exaltation in the highest degree. The exaltation of Christ is such that at the name of Jesus every knee is summoned to bow. Every tongue is called upon to confess. The faithlessness of the contemporary Church is seen precisely in this. The Church, on the basis of various doctrinal *excuses,* has taken to granting exemptions and has been doing this contrary to what she was expressly told to declare. Just as the medieval church used to sell indulgences for various sins, so the modern churches grant indulgences to magistrates, saying, "You don't *really* have to acknowledge that Jesus is Lord."

Every knee and every tongue includes every knee and tongue in the White House and in Congress. It includes all nine tongues on the Supreme Court and all eighteen knees. Our corrupted justices are hereby told, in the name of Jesus Christ, that they have been summoned. They answer to an authority beyond them, an authority which is *far* beyond them. This encompasses the General Assembly of the U.N. and the entire future of mankind.

We do not declare anything in order to make it so. We declare it because God has already made it so. The Great Commission is not the process of giving Jesus authority. The Great Commission is the process of declaring the authority that He *already* possesses and which He is *already* wielding by and through our preaching and worship.

The Christian faith is a public faith. The claims of Jesus Christ are absolute, and we have no authority to diminish the authority that God has given to Him to make these claims. We may not say, of any name, that *it* has the right to refuse to acknowledge that the name of Jesus is the ultimate authority. No one, standing at the last judgment, will have the right to say that he *would* have acknowledged the authority of Jesus, but certain key interpretations of the First Amendment prohibited it. At that great day, when the sky and earth have fled to hide themselves, they will not be authorized to appeal to Jefferson's "wall of separation" between church and state. There is no wall of separation between the authority of Jesus Christ and the authority of the civil magistrate. American Christians must come to grips with this. There will be no salvation for our nation without a Savior. And because there is a Savior, then our nation, along with all the others, *will* be saved.

Many Christians want to avoid millennial† wrangles, and in an important sense, they are quite right. It makes little sense to fight with one another about when the divine *peace* will come. But other Christians want to avoid debate on the subject because they believe it to be trivial or unimportant. "After all, is not the 'millennium' found only in chapter twenty of the book of Revelation, a notoriously difficult chapter in a notoriously difficult book? Shouldn't we just walk away from it?" If we were limited to the word *millennium,* this might have some weight. But what happens when we consider the word *kingdom?* As we have just seen, Christ is the king before whom all must bow, but doesn't this require a kingdom?

† **millennial:** *referring to the one thousand years of peace prophesied by the apostle John in Revelation 20.*

> From that time Jesus began to preach and to say, "Repent, for the kingdom of heaven is at hand.". . . And Jesus went about all Galilee, teaching in their synagogues, preaching the gospel of the kingdom, and healing all kinds of sickness and all kinds of disease among the people. (Mt. 4:17, 23; cf. 9:35)

A central duty of the Christian church is that of preaching the kingdom. And the kingdom of God is an immense subject—as great as the love of God, which is to say, as great as the gospel. A central theme in scriptural references to the kingdom is the way that history will develop until the King returns. This means our gospel preaching must contain that historical element if it is to be biblical. But how often do modern Christian evangelists preach the *kingdom?*

We have a kingdom gospel, and so we ought to be preaching a kingdom gospel.

And this *gospel of the kingdom* will be preached in all the world as a witness to all the nations, and then the end will come. (Mt. 24:14)

We also find repentance tied to the proclamation of the kingdom.

In those days John the Baptist came preaching in the wilderness of Judea, and saying, "Repent, for the kingdom of heaven is at hand!" (Mt. 3:2)

The New Testament contains kingdom teaching. Knowledge of the kingdom was central to the Lord's discipleship of His followers after the resurrection, and He certainly expected them to continue that theme with those whom they came to instruct.

[T]o whom He also presented Himself alive after His suffering by many infallible proofs, being seen by them during forty days and speaking of the things *pertaining to the kingdom of God.* (Acts 1:3)

Not surprisingly, there is also kingdom preaching, royal proclamation.

But when they believed Philip as he *preached* the things *concerning the kingdom of God* and the name of Jesus Christ, both men and women were baptized. (Acts 8:12; cf. 20:25; 28:31)

And there is kingdom apologetics. New Testament apologetics was about the meaning and direction of history, and was not about the kind of thing that comes up in philosophy classes.

And he went into the synagogue and spoke boldly for three months, *reasoning* and *persuading* concerning the things of *the kingdom of God.* (Acts 19:8)

So what is this kingdom then? The kingdom of God is nothing less than the *rule* and *realm* of the Lord Jesus Christ, manifested in history according to His will and pleasure. Is He not the king? Is this not how we pray? "Your kingdom come. Your will be done on earth as it is in heaven" (Mt. 6:10).

We are not taught to pray, "Your kingdom *go.*" We are not taught to pray that God's will would be done in heaven when we eventually get there. We pray for God's will to be done *on earth* as it already is in heaven. God's good pleasure is to have His kingdom start really small and gradually grow to fill the earth.

> Another parable He put forth to them, saying: "The kingdom of heaven is like a mustard seed, which a man took and sowed in his field, which indeed is the least of all the seeds; but when it is grown it is greater than the herbs and becomes a tree, so that the birds of the air come and nest in its branches." (Mt. 13:31–32)

When the kingdom has grown to its appointed size, the Lord will come.

> Then comes the end, when He delivers the kingdom to God the Father, when He puts an end to all rule and all authority and power. For He must reign till He has put all enemies under His feet. The last enemy that will be destroyed is death. (1 Cor. 15:24–26)

But doesn't the Bible say that the way of salvation is narrow? How can the kingdom of God fill the earth then? As attractive as all this may sound, aren't there contrary verses in the Bible? Yes, the Bible does contain passages which look contrary—at first glance. This would include passages like, "Narrow is the way" (Mt. 7:14). But we need to learn the ways of the kingdom.

Consider Luke 13:22–30. The narrow gate was for the remnant of the Jews of the first century, and then immediately after, in that same passage, the Gentiles would *stream in.* In another place, Jesus teaches the Jews, "Therefore I say to you, the kingdom of God will be taken from you and given to a nation bearing the fruits of it" (Mt. 21:43). When Jesus said that the way was narrow, and that only few would find it, He was speaking specifically about first century Judaism. From that body of people, only a remnant was saved, and then the Gentiles poured in. We see this again when Jesus makes the same narrow claim in Matthew 8: "And I say to you that many will come from east and west, and sit down with Abraham, Isaac, and Jacob in the kingdom of heaven" (Mt. 8:11). This great kingdom is not an earthly kingdom established by carnal rule. It is not just another kingdom, but a different kind of kingdom altogether. "[N]ow My kingdom is not from here" (Jn. 18:36). And we must always remember the demeanor and character of its citizens. The fact that the kingdom is not "from here" does not make it ethereal. Rather, this kingdom operates on the foundation of sacrifice, instead of the foundation of grasping, which is characteristic of the kingdoms of men.

> Therefore do not let your good be spoken of as evil; for the kingdom of God is not eating and drinking, but righteousness and peace and joy in the Holy Spirit. (Rom. 14:16–17)

And of course, we rejoice in the gift we have been given—a kingdom which cannot be shaken.

> Therefore, since we are receiving a kingdom which cannot be shaken, let us have grace, by which we may serve God acceptably with reverence and godly fear. For our God is a consuming fire. (Heb. 12:28)

Questions for Discussion

The Bible teaches that Christ has been given a name that is above every other name. It is important to note that this was not limited to those nations that don't have a "separation of church and state."

1. If Jesus has been given a name above every name, what are the implications for the public square in secularist societies? Do cultures have a *right* to be secular?
2. What does it mean to preach "the kingdom." When modern preachers preach "the gospel" are they also preaching the kingdom?
3. What does Jesus mean when He says the way is "narrow"? Discuss.

9.

THEREFORE GO

The Greatness of the Great Commission

Jesus did not tell us to go and disciple the nations. He told us to *therefore* go.

> And Jesus came and spake unto them, saying, All power is given unto me in heaven and in earth. Go ye therefore, and teach all nations, baptizing them in the name of the Father, and of the Son, and of the Holy Ghost: teaching them to observe all things whatsoever I have commanded you: and lo, I am with you always, even unto the end of the world. Amen. (Mt. 28:18–20)

Our understanding of the basis of the command affects our understanding of the command itself. In this Scripture Jesus says that He has all power (or authority), and He has this authority because it was *given* to Him.

He has this authority in heaven, and He has this authority on earth. Not only is this the case, but He says that He has *all* authority in heaven and on earth. There is now no authority in heaven or on earth that is not subordinate to His authority. This includes, but is not limited to, the United States Supreme Court, the Muslim rulers of Saudi Arabia, every parliament on the continent of Europe, the United Nations General Assembly, the U.S. Congress, the legislature of South Dakota, the communist thugs running North Korea, every secret meeting ever convened by the Illuminati or whoever those guys are, and the commissioner of baseball.

Now if this is the reason given for the command, it makes sense that our understanding of this principle, or our neglect of it, will affect our obedience to the command. If we begin with *all* authority, we end with *all* nations. If we begin with an invisible and very spiritual authority, then we end with small collections, in every nation, of believers in this invisible and very spiritual authority. But Jesus did not want a small collection of struggling churches *in* Pakistan; He wants Pakistan itself. He is happy to begin with the small beachhead in an unbelieving nation, but that beachhead must not confuse itself with the coming occupation.

But Jesus Christ has not commanded His church to do the impossible. And we should note that we are not commanded to give everyone in the world a *chance* to be saved—we were told to *disciple the nations*. This is the earthly task of the church, and nothing else is. The apostle Paul makes the same point at the end of Romans.

> Now to Him who is able to establish you according to my gospel and the preaching of Jesus Christ, according to the revelation of the mystery kept secret since the world began but now has been made manifest, and by the prophetic Scriptures *has been made known to all nations,* according to the commandment of the everlasting God, *for obedience to the faith*—to God, alone wise, be glory through Jesus Christ forever. Amen. (Rom. 16:25–27)

The reason the gospel has now been revealed to the nations is so that they would come to the obedience of the faith. This is what God commands them to do. The Church is commanded to preach it, the world is commanded to believe it, and the Church is commanded to preach it *until* the world believes it.

So Jesus didn't say "go." He said to *therefore go*. This authority that the command rests on is crucial to our understanding of the Great Commission. But it is also important for us to remember that Jesus was not just making this up as He went along. He lived on the basis of His absolute faith that the Word of God could not be broken, and His declaration that He had all authority was founded on numerous passages in the Old Testament.

In various places, including at His trial, Jesus mentioned Himself as the Son of Man, coming on the clouds of heaven. This is easily thought to be a reference to the Second Coming, and since the Second Coming has not happened yet, at least not by the time this book went to print, then it must be awaiting a future fulfillment. What else could "coming on the clouds of heaven" mean? Well, the question can best be answered by looking at the passage that Jesus was quoting when He said it.

> I saw in the night visions, and behold, one like the Son of man came with the clouds of heaven, *and came to the Ancient of days,* and they brought him near before him. *And there was given him dominion,* and glory, and a kingdom, that all people, nations, and languages, should serve him: his dominion is an everlasting dominion, which shall not pass away, and his kingdom that which shall not be destroyed. (Dan. 7:13–14).

When Jesus applied this to Himself, He was not describing the Second Coming, but rather the Ascension. And after His Ascension and enthronement, His first great authoritative act was to decree the destruction of Jerusalem, which those who pierced Him *saw.* The "coming on clouds" is the time when the Son of Man came into the throne room of the Almighty, the Ancient of Days, and was there given universal dominion. Jesus knew that this was going to be His, and He knew this on the basis of what the prophets had spoken. And on that basis He told His disciples to preach the gospel to all the nations.

When the Son of Man comes in the clouds of heaven, He is presented to the Ancient of Days. Authority was then given to Him— described as dominion, glory, and a kingdom. And lest we interpret this as dominion, glory and a kingdom in some invisible spiritual place, the prophecy goes on to tell us what the result of that establishment would be. The result was that *all* people, nations and languages would serve Him. When Jesus said that all authority in heaven and earth had been given to Him, this is what He was talking about. And His dominion, once established, would be an everlasting dominion. It could not come to an end. This means that when Jesus told His disciples about His authority, He was not talking about a temporary or provisional authority. It would last to the day of resurrection at the end of the world, when the kingdom would be given back to God. The kingdom would not fade away or be destroyed—which is not something that any other kingdom in the history of the human race can say.

Now this understanding radically affects what we are doing when we seek to fulfill the Great Commission. Are we trying to *do* something, or are we telling the world about what has *already* been done? Are we fighting the principal battle itself, or are we announcing the victory afterwards?

This is not a campaign where we are trying to get Jesus elected to anything. He is seated already at the right hand of God the Father, and He is already the king of Idaho, Virginia, Maryland, and Massachusetts. We have the task of announcing to the remaining rebels in the hinterlands that their capital city has already fallen, their ruler dethroned, and that resistance is futile.

This is what it means to *therefore go.* Jesus already has all authority and we are not trying to get any more for Him. On the basis of this established authority, we are to preach to the nations and announce to them their responsibility to submit to the authority of the Lord Jesus.

So in the night visions, Daniel sees someone like the Son of man coming on the clouds of heaven (v. 13). The one like the Son of man approaches the Ancient of days (God the Father), and is brought before Him (v. 13). When this mysterious figure approaches the Ancient of days, the end result is that universal dominion is bestowed on him—dominion, glory, and a kingdom. The nature of this kingdom was that all people, nations, and languages would serve him (v. 14). His dominion is to be everlasting, and the kingdom he has received will never be destroyed (v. 14). Preaching the kingdom of God, among other things, means preaching *this.* Now we do still preach a gospel of individual, personal repentance, faith, and piety. We do still very clearly know the difference between a nation where Jesus is King and it is not acknowledged, and a nation where it is acknowledged. And the victory of this kingdom is still watered by the blood of the martyrs, figuratively and literally: the way of the cross is still the only way to enduring glory.

The first thing to note is how Jesus identifies with this phrase—"the Son of man." Although the phrase is common in the Old Testament, this is the only passage in the entire Old Testament where it is used in a messianic† sense. Thus, it is a messianic term, but not a common one. The Lord Jesus uses it, and it simultaneously conceals and reveals His identity. Some common examples would include Mark 2:10, 8:38, and 10:33. The Lord did not want His disciples proclaiming His identity until the time was right. After His resurrection and ascension

† **messianic:** *relating to the promised and awaited deliverer of old Israel.*

(Rom. 1:4) the time was more than right, and so this reality now must be declared until the end of the world. This is what we are charged to declare—Christ's universal lordship over (and consequent salvation of) the entire world. Salvation of the world doesn't mean salvation of each and every person. But it does mean salvation of the world.

We must let the Bible tell us what this phrase means. When we think of "the Son of man coming on the clouds of heaven," what do we think? We almost always think of the Second Coming, with Jesus descending to earth. But this is not what it means at all.

The fact that Jesus ascended into heaven on the clouds (the event the Church commemorates on Ascension Day) is not meant (with regard to this prophecy) to point to another event many thousands of years later. Although Jesus will come again the same way He left, His manner of going was the beginning of the fulfillment itself.

> And when he had spoken these things, while they beheld, he was taken up; *and a cloud received him* out of their sight. And while they looked stedfastly toward heaven as he went up, behold, two men stood by them in white apparel; Which also said, Ye men of Galilee, why stand ye gazing up into heaven? this same Jesus, which is taken up from you into heaven, *shall so come in like manner as ye have seen him go* into heaven. (Acts 1:9–11)

The Jews who put Jesus on trial understood the ramifications of this phrase better than many modern Christians do. This is why, tearing his clothes, the high priest considered the statement blasphemous.

Jesus saith unto him, Thou hast said: nevertheless I say unto you, Hereafter shall ye see the Son of man sitting on the right hand of power, and coming in the clouds of heaven. Then the high priest rent his clothes, saying, He hath spoken blasphemy; what further need have we of witnesses? behold, now ye have heard his blasphemy. (Mt. 26:64–65; cf. Mk. 14:62–64)

We should pay close attention to it—for this was the passage that brought about the conviction of Jesus.

Returning to Daniel, what did the Lord Jesus receive after He departed from the disciples' sight in a cloud? What did He receive when He approached the Ancient of days? The Scriptures are exceedingly clear on the point. He received everlasting dominion, glory, and an indestructible and universal kingdom (Dan. 7:13–14). He received the heathen for His inheritance and the uttermost ends of the earth as His possession (Ps. 2:8). He receives the worship of all the families on earth and the remembrance of all the ends of the world (Ps. 22:27). He will receive all men as they stream to Him, the ensign of Jesse (Is. 11:10), and His rest shall be glorious. The earth will be as full of the knowledge of the Lord Jesus as the Pacific is wet (Is. 11:9). He will receive all His adversaries, made into His footstool (Ps. 110:1). He will receive the human race, unveiled (Is. 25:7), and will set a feast of fat things, full of marrow, full of fat, and wine on the lees, well-refined (Is. 25:8).

This world, the one we live in *now*, will be put to rights, *before* the Second Coming, *before* the end of all things. The only enemy not destroyed through the advance of the gospel will be death itself (1 Cor. 15:26)—and even *that* enemy will be in confused retreat (Is. 65:20). The ramifications of this are many, but one of the things it means is that your labor in the Lord is not in vain.

Jesus came to establish the kingdom of God, and this kingdom was not a new idea. Neither was the sure understanding about the nature of its growth.

And in the days of these kings the God of heaven will set up a kingdom which shall never be destroyed; and the kingdom shall not be left to other people; it shall break in pieces and consume all these kingdoms, and it shall stand forever. Inasmuch as you saw that the stone was cut out of the mountain without hands, and that it broke in pieces the iron, the bronze, the clay, the silver, and the gold—the great God has made known to the king what will come to pass after this. The dream is certain, and its interpretation is sure. (Dan. 2:44–45)

As the vision makes clear, the stone in question, which is the kingdom of God, grows gradually until it fills the whole earth. The dream is certain and its interpretation is sure.

The point, made again and again in the Old Testament, was not at all lost on the writers of the New Testament. At the council of Jerusalem, the brother of the Lord says this.

After this I will return and will rebuild the tabernacle of David, which has fallen down; I will rebuild its ruins, and I will set it up; so that the rest of mankind may seek the LORD, even all the Gentiles who are called by My name, says the LORD who does all these things. (Acts 15:16–17)

This citation of Amos by James is one of the mildest expressions of this expectation in the New Testament. But even here the "rest of mankind" will seek the Lord. The expectation is well-grounded and pervasive.

Questions for Discussion

The Great Commission has been rightly described as giving the "marching orders" of the Church. If this is the case, we have to be very careful that we understand what it is that Jesus told us to do.

1. What is the difference between gathering disciples out of every nation and discipling every nation?
2. What is the difference between "go" and "therefore go"?
3. Do we give Christ authority by fulfilling the Great Commission? Why or why not?

10.

ALL ENDS OF EARTH

What Was on the Lord's Mind as He Died?

The transition between the old age and the new was accomplished in Christ—in the death, burial, and resurrection of Christ. Because He has now ascended to the right hand of God the Father, human history has been utterly transformed. We can see the potency of this transition in Psalm 22, which contains one of the great Old Testament portrayals of the gospel. Along with Isaiah 53, we learn here that the death of Christ for the sins of the world was no afterthought. The Lamb of God was indeed slain from before the foundations of the world. All this is what Abraham saw. And this is what the Psalmist saw as well.

> My God, my God, why hast thou forsaken me? why art thou so far from helping me, and from the words of my roaring? O my God, I cry in the daytime, but thou hearest not; and in the night season, and am not silent. (Ps. 22:1–31)

Christ cries out, forsaken by His Father (v. 1). He receives no answer (v. 2), and yet He knows that God, the One who inhabits Israel's praises, is holy (v. 3). Our fathers cried out to God, and *they* were heard (vv. 4–5). But the Lord, at least for the present, is in a different place. They despise Him (vv. 6–7), and they taunt Him for His faith (v. 8). The response of the Lord Jesus is to remind Himself of His life-long faith in God (vv. 9–10). He then renews His request for God to deliver (vv. 11, 19). Between these two verses, we see how desperate His circumstances were—He was surrounded by threatening bulls (vv. 12–13), He was poured out like water and His bones were out of joint (v. 14), His heart is like wax (v. 14), His strength is dried like a potsherd and He is brought down to the dust of death (v. 15), dogs have surrounded Him, and His hands and feet are pierced (v. 16), He can count his bones (v. 17), and gamblers compete for His clothing (v. 18). His cry for deliverance resumes—He cries out to be saved from the lion and the unicorn (vv. 20–21).

The second half of the psalm is the triumphant cry of faith, which is what follows His great despairing cry *of faith.* He will praise God in the congregation (v. 22). All who fear God are summoned to join in the praise (v. 23). Why is this? God answers the prayer of the faithful, *including this one* (v. 24). Christ shall praise God in the great congregation (v. 25). The meek (who will inherit the earth) shall also eat and be satisfied (v. 26). *All the ends of the earth shall be converted and turn to the Lord,* and they will worship Him (v. 27). The Lord has conquered the world through His faithful despairing (v. 28). Rich and poor alike shall serve Him (v. 29), and the Lord shall have His posterity, which will be a glorious posterity (v. 30). And they will testify that the Lord has done this (v. 31).

An ancient Christian tradition held that Christ on the cross began quoting Psalm 22 here, and He did not stop quoting the Psalter until He came to Psalm 31:5—"into thine hand I commit my spirit." Although we cannot assert this dogmatically, this certainly accords with what is happening here. This moment on the cross is the fulfillment of *all* God's purposes, expressed so clearly throughout the entire Old Testament, and most particularly in this psalm. A man would have to be blind (and sadly many are) not to see how all these ancient words are coming to a glorious fruition.

The words of this psalm were written about a thousand years before Christ. We are not only talking about what Abraham saw but about what David saw as well. And chronologically David was to Christ what William the Conqueror is to us. One thousand years before it all happened, David saw, through the Spirit, that Christ's hands and feet were to be pierced (v. 16), that He would die at the hands of His enemies (vv. 12–13, 16), that His clothing would be gambled for (v. 18), and that He would die in agony (vv. 15, 17). We are Christians, so we believe all of this. But what of the rest of the psalm? For those of us who stumble in our faith, we are told that all of these things, taken together, *will conquer the world* (v. 27). As surely as the nails went into Christ's hands, just as surely all the ends of the earth will become Christian. Further, all these details of Christ's death were itemized in prophecy, and wicked men *blindly fulfilled all of it*, thinking themselves to be lords of the earth (1 Cor. 2:8; Jn. 12:32).

There are many reasons to take the malice of these wicked men seriously. They are described here as raging (very powerful) bulls. They gape with their mouths in a terrifying way. The dogs are set loose, and the image is that of a hunted animal, like a stag, at bay. Ravening dogs surround the Lord's victim. And they do more than threaten. The Lord falls into their hands—everything is going their way. They mock Him, but they also pierce Him. They win, and they taunt as though they have won. They have the power of bulls, of ravening dogs, of a rampaging lion, of a vaunting unicorn. They exult as they hang the Messiah of God upon a gibbet, and lift Him up . . . and by their wicked action *they accomplished the salvation of the entire world*. Their murdering malice was the instrument of my salvation, and yours, and not ours only, but also the salvation of all the ends of the earth.

We here see Christ forsaken by the Father. This is not to say that the Trinity unraveled, but rather that the unbroken fellowship between God and His incarnate Son was disrupted. This is not a cry of despairing faith, but rather a cry of faithful despair. When Christ experiences this abandonment by the Father, He quotes Scripture; it is still, "*My* God, *my* God," and the psalm continues, expressing that though He hung on the cross, Christ had the glorious vision of God's triumph right in front of Him. The ends of the earth *will* turn, and the joy set before Him was glorious (Heb. 12:2).

What is it that accomplishes this? "For he hath made him to be sin for us, who knew no sin; that we might be made the righteousness of God in him" (2 Cor. 5:21). On the cross, Christ's faith threw down all despair, sin, rebellion, and wickedness. And because Christ died as the perfect substitute for His people, He has conquered the world.

Questions for Discussion

When Christ died on the cross, He did so knowing that He was going to come back from the dead. He did not know this because He was secretly accessing the knowledge. He knew this because God had promised that this is what He would do throughout the Old Testament. He had been singing and chanting the psalms since He was a small boy. God had published the game plan in advance.

1. When Christ cried out in despair on the cross, what was the significance of the passage He chose to quote?
2. How does Psalm 22 begin? How does it end? Did Jesus know?
3. What does the crucifixion of Christ tell us about the opposition of sinful men to the gospel?

11.

LEARNING TO READ THE PROMISES

Tutorial Help from the Apostles

Wouldn't it be wonderful to be able to take a class from one of the apostles on how to read Scripture? To able to sit across the table from the apostle Paul or Peter and have them explain to you what these dense passages in Isaiah are actually talking about?

In this short book we've presented, what is for many, a very different way of looking at the Scriptures. We've discussed historical optimism, as opposed to the very common historical pessimism found in the modern evangelical world.

If we learn to read the Bible from what the apostles left to us, one of the immediate blessings (as far as this subject is concerned) will be that we know what to do with numerous passages that currently leave us scratching our heads.

One of the things virtually all Christians notice as they read through the New Testament is the pervasive expectation of "the Day." When this is coupled with the assumption that the passages are all talking about the end of the world, such references become a problem because here we are two thousand years later, and it still hasn't happened. Why does the New Testament sound so urgent if the fulfillment of these statements was still thousands of years off? Have you ever wondered why we are all still here, and still alive, when the New Testament says things like this? Be honest.

Assuredly, I say to you, *this generation* will by no means pass away till all these things take place. (Mt. 24:34)

When they persecute you in this city, flee to another. For assuredly, I say to you, *you* will not have gone through the cities of Israel *before the Son of Man comes.* (Mt. 10:23)

[N]ot forsaking the assembling of ourselves together, as is the manner of some, but exhorting one another, and so much the more as *you see* the Day approaching. (Heb. 10:25)

You also be patient. Establish your hearts, for *the coming of the Lord is at hand.* Do not grumble against one another, brethren, lest you be condemned. Behold, *the Judge is standing at the door!* (Jas. 5:8–9)

Little children, *it is the last hour;* and as you have heard that the Antichrist is coming, even now many antichrists have come, by which *we know that it is the last hour.* (1 Jn. 2:18)

The Revelation of Jesus Christ, which God gave Him to show His servants—things *which must shortly take place.* And He sent and signified it by His angel to His servant John. (Rev. 1:1)

Blessed is he who reads and those who hear the words of this prophecy, and keep those things which are written in it; for *the time is near.* (Rev. 1:3)

Behold, I am coming *quickly!* Hold fast what you have, that no one may take your crown. (Rev. 3:11)

Behold, I am coming *quickly!* Blessed is he who keeps the words of the prophecy of this book. (Rev. 22:7)

And behold, I am coming *quickly,* and My reward is with Me, to give to every one according to his work. (Rev. 22:12)

He who testifies to these things says, "Surely I am coming *quickly.*" Amen. Even so, come, Lord Jesus! (Rev. 22:20)*

---

*In this context, "quickly" does not mean "suddenly" but rather "soon" and "imminently."

None of these passages would lead us to think that we need to wait two thousand years or more. When confronted with these passages (and there are many more), the reader of the New Testament has basically three options. First, he can take the route of unbelieving liberalism, and say that the New Testament writers expected to see a spectacular end to the world in their day, and that they were sadly mistaken. Second, he can say that the expectation was not fulfilled because the prophecies somehow refer to the end of the world. But then the natural meaning of the words indicating its nearness in time must be "spiritualized." Third, we can say that the writers of the New Testament expected to see these things come to pass in their day, *and they were correct.* Their expectations were fulfilled. Reading this way is one of the fruits of letting the first-century apostles tell us what a passage means.

Picture the Old Testament on a single sheet of paper, rolled out on a work bench in front of you. Then take the New Testament as a transparent overlay, and roll it out on top of the Old Testament. Then—if you would learn from Jesus and the apostles—take a nail and drive it through both testaments at every place where the New Testament fixes the meaning of the Old. This occurs in many places, and it is not long before you can begin to pick up on the patterns.

When I was first working through this, I bought a Bible I could mark up well. I then spent a few weeks looking up every passage in the Old Testament that is quoted in the New. Many Bibles will mark such cross-references in the New Testament, but it is rarely done in the Old. I highlighted every quotation from the Old Testament in the New Testament, and then I looked it up in the Old Testament and highlighted it there. Then I wrote in the Old Testament margin where in the New Testament this passage was quoted. When I was done, I had sloppily executed The Apostolic Study Bible. When I was reading in the Old Testament, I could immediately tell if Jesus, Peter, or Paul had ever discussed the passage I was currently wondering about. I would then look at what they said, and the striking thing is that they were consistently surprising. They *often* said the passage I was reading was not about what I had thought it was.

So our pattern should be that of allowing the New Testament to provide commentary on what passages in the Old Testament mean. We must learn how to read Scripture as disciples. For the apostles not only teach us about Jesus; they also teach us about Deuteronomy. They also teach us how to read the Bible. And, on the subject we are currently considering, they teach us how to think about the future of our world.

Let's consider a few examples. Because our subject is historical optimism, we will be looking at places which deal with this particular subject, but the process involved should govern all our studies. We should strive to allow the New Testament to teach us the Old Testament. Let the Bible teach the Bible. In the exercise I described just a moment ago, I also discovered the "favorite" books of the New Testament writers. More often quoted than anything else were Genesis, Deuteronomy, Psalms, and Isaiah. So let's consider a text from each on the future of our world.

In Genesis, as we noted in chapter two, God made some spectacular promises to Abraham.

> Get thee out of thy country . . . and I will make thee a great nation . . . in thee shall all families of the earth be blessed. (Gen. 12:1–2)

> And he brought him forth abroad, and said, Look now towards heaven, and tell the stars, if thou be able to number them. And he said unto him, So shall thy seed be. And he believed in the LORD; and he counted it to him for righteousness. (Gen. 15:5–6)

> And I will make my covenant between me and thee, and will multiply thee exceedingly. (Gen. 17:2)

Now the procedure here is simple. We should let the New Testament tell us what this all means.

> For the promise that he should be the *heir of the world*, was not to Abraham, or to his seed, through the law, but through the righteousness of faith. (Rom. 4:13)

We who believe are the seed of Abraham, as the New Testament teaches in many places. We will inherit the world together with

Abraham, and we will do this—not through the law—but by the righteousness of faith. What is it that overcomes the world? It is our faith. We are called, not only to believe in God, in the way that Abraham did, but to believe what he believed. And what did he believe? He believed that God promised him the world. He did not promise heaven by and by—although Abraham is in heaven. He promised him the *world,* and we who believe are the instrument of that fulfillment. We think we're looking forward to some spiritualized city called the New Jerusalem. But so was Abraham according to Hebrews 11:10, and what Abraham was looking forward to (according to Romans 4:13) was nothing less than the whole world. Therefore, the New Jerusalem encompasses the whole world.

Then there is Deuteronomy. Through Moses God promised the people of Israel a prophet like Moses. This promise was quoted by Stephen in Acts 7:37 and applied to Christ. Acts 3:22–23 makes the same identification, but with a little bit more information.

> Jesus Christ . . . whom heaven must receive until the times of restoration of all things, which God has spoken by the mouth of all His holy prophets since the world began. For Moses truly said to the fathers, "The Lord your God will raise up for you a Prophet like me from your brethren. Him you shall hear in all things, whatever He says to you. And it shall be that every soul who will not hear that Prophet shall be utterly destroyed from among the people." Yes, and all the prophets, from Samuel and those who follow, as many as have spoken, *have also foretold these days.* You are sons of the prophets, and of the covenant which God made with our fathers, saying to Abraham, "And in your seed all the families of the earth shall be blessed." To you first, God, having raised up His Servant Jesus, sent Him to bless you, in turning away every one of you from your iniquities. (Acts 3:20–26)

This is important. We are told here that all the prophecies were about "these days." These fulfillments will not begin to come to pass in our future, but rather began to be fulfilled two thousand years ago.

This passage contains both a command and a promise. The command involves individual accountability for sin—"repent and be converted." We see that the engine which drives this optimistic hope is not some falsely optimistic view of human nature, but rather confidence in the efficacy of the gospel to overcome depraved human nature. In the gospel, God *deals* with sin. Notice that we are told here what the reference point is for *all* the Old Testament prophecies; it is "these days." We are told that Moses prophesied this gospel era, and all the prophets, from Samuel on, were talking about *this same thing.*

Psalm 2 is quoted in multiple places in the New Testament (Acts 4:25–26; 13:33; Heb. 1:5; 5:5; Rev. 2:27; 19:15), and the psalm only has twelve verses. The first two are quoted in Acts 4 and applied to the crucifixion. This would be an example of one of those nails— drive it through Acts 4:25–26 and into Psalm 2:1–2, and you *know* that the first words of this psalm are about the crucifixion of Jesus.

> Why do the heathen rage, and the people imagine a vain thing? The kings of the earth set themselves, and the rulers take counsel together, against the LORD, and against his anointed, saying, Let us break their bands asunder. (Ps. 2:1–3a)

God's response to this vain attempt against His sovereign work of salvation is one of laughter. He then declares Himself concerning His Son. Verse 7 is quoted three times in the New Testament, and in each instance, the reference is to Christ's *becoming* something after His completed work. And Acts 13:33 makes this explicitly about the resurrection.

> God hath fulfilled the same unto us their children, in that *he hath raised up Jesus* again, *as it is also written in the second psalm,* Thou art my Son, this day have I begotten thee.

The New Testament makes this statement ("this day have I begotten thee") about the resurrection from the dead—Christ is the firstborn from the dead.

Now, in verse 8, right after the resurrection, Christ is given the nations.

> Ask of me, and I shall give thee the heathen for thy inheritance, and the uttermost parts of the earth for thy possession. (Ps. 2:8)

Not to put too fine a point on it, the reason that we believe that Christ owns all the nations now is that the Father invited Him *to ask for them* immediately following the resurrection. Why would the Lord purchase all the nations with His blood and then not ask for them? Jesus knew that this request was granted because He knew that all authority in heaven and on earth *had been given to Him* (Mt. 28:18).

We also see this in verse 9 of this psalm being quoted twice in Revelation. The first time Christ shares His authority with those believers who overcome, and the second time it is applied to Christ alone.

> And he that overcometh, and keepeth my works unto the end, to him will I give *power over the nations:* and he shall rule them with *a rod of iron;* as the vessels of a potter shall they be broken to shivers: *even as I received of my Father.* (Rev. 2:26–27; cf. Rev. 19:15)

Jesus has been given all authority by His Father, and He shares that authority with those who believe in Him.

The psalm concludes with an appeal to the kings of the earth to make their peace with the Christ. "Kiss the Son, lest He be angry." The upshot of the psalm is that all the world's political rulers are commanded to become Christians and to bring their glory and honor into the New Jerusalem. Jesus asked for the nations as a gift, and He has received what He has asked for (Rev. 21:24).

Let's take another quick example from the psalms. Psalm 110 is also quoted many times in the New Testament (Mt: 22:44; Mk. 12:36; Lk. 20:42–43; Acts 2:34–35; Heb. 1:13; 5:6; 7:17, 21). The psalm ends with Christ crushing the rulers of the whole earth. But how is this to be done? In the gospels Christ quotes the psalm to show that David's Lord is also David's son. But in Acts 2:33–35, the passage is applied to the *present reign* of Christ at the right hand of the Father. The rest of the quotations refer to Him as both prince and priest in terms of a present reality. This means that He will remain at God's right hand *until* His gospel work is accomplished.

What about Isaiah? The great vision of glory and peace is given in Isaiah 11, and we know it well. The lion will lie down with the lamb.

They shall not hurt nor destroy in all My holy mountain, for the earth shall be full of the knowledge of the LORD as the waters cover the sea. *And in that day* there shall be a Root of Jesse, Who shall stand as a banner to the people; for the Gentiles shall seek Him, and His resting place shall be glorious. (Is. 11:9–10)

But when will this happen? Let the New Testament tell us. Remember that Paul quotes this in Romans 15:12.

Now I say that Jesus Christ has become a servant to the circumcision for the truth of God, to confirm the promises made to the fathers, and that the Gentiles might glorify God for His mercy, as it is written . . . And again, Isaiah says: "There shall be a root of Jesse; and He who shall rise to reign over the Gentiles, in Him the Gentiles shall hope." (Rom. 15:8–9, 12)

Simply put, Paul tells us that Isaiah's vision began to come to fruition in his day, in Paul's mission to the Gentiles, which was two thousand years ago.

Questions for Discussion
When we want to learn how to handle the Scriptures, one of the first things we should do is turn to the apostles. They interpreted the Old Testament all the time. We should take lessons from them.

1. What were the New Testament writers' favorite books in the Old Testament? How can we tell?
2. In what way can the New Testament set boundaries for us as we seek to interpret Old Testament passages?
3. How do we know that Psalm 2 contains prophecies of both the crucifixion and the resurrection? What are the implications for the fulfillment of the Great Commission?

12.

AND THE STARS FELL OUT OF THE SKY

Leftover Bits from the Old Way of Thinking, Part 1

The words of Christ in Matthew 24 have caused far more consternation and confusion than they should have. The key, as we learned in the previous chapter, is to look at how the passages quoted from the Old Testament are used in the New Testament and then at how the events of the first century actually unfolded.

> Then Jesus went out and departed from the temple, and His disciples came up to show Him the buildings of the temple. And Jesus said to them, "Do you not see all these things? Assuredly, I say to you, not one stone shall be left here upon another, that shall not be thrown down." (Mt. 24:1–2)

The first thing to do is place the prophecy. When we seek to understand where this prophecy should be placed in time, we should look for direct teaching in the passage on it. And fortunately, that is what we find.

Jesus told the disciples that not one stone would be left on another (vv. 1–2). This statement prompts the disciples to ask a series of questions. Now, the way they are usually read, they appear to be detached and unrelated questions. "When will this happen? And when will a bunch of *other* things happen?" But it is far more natural to take their questions as relating to the same series of events—the destruction of the temple, the sign of Christ's coming (in judgment on Jerusalem), and the sign of the end of the (Judaic) age. This—the natural flow of conversation—is one time indicator.

The second indication is the phrase "this generation." Using a "literal" means of interpretation, how are we to understand Jesus' words in verse 34: "Assuredly, I say to you, this generation will by no means pass away till all these things take place"? Let us take His words at face value—all those things which He mentioned prior to verse 34 would occur within a generation (i.e., within about forty years). This would bring us to the culminating events of A.D. 70, when the Romans leveled Jerusalem.

But . . . how is this possible? When we read about some of those things mentioned prior to verse 34, and then go outside and look at the sky, we see that they appear *not* to have taken place. Scoffers have frequently seized on this point, thinking that Christ was obviously wrong about when the end of the world would be. But the problem is that *He was not talking about the end of the world at all.* He was not asked about the end of the space/time continuum. He was asked about the destruction of Jerusalem, and He answered the question. He was speaking about *the end of the age of Israel.*

Here are some key questions. If we believe that our Lord requires us to place His words in the first century, how is this to be understood without doing violence to the text?

First, consider the phrase the "end is not yet." The first series of troubles (vv. 3–13) in this passage are commonly cited as signs of the end. This is curious, because Jesus mentioned them in order to tell us that they did *not* mean that the end had arrived. Wars and rumors of wars mean that we should *not* be worried.

Next, we should note the "witness to the nations." The gospel was to go forth, and was to be proclaimed under heaven. And then the end would come. Did this happen? The Bible says *yes.* Note that this witness is not the same thing as fulfillment of the Great Commission.

> First, I thank my God through Jesus Christ for you all, that your
> faith is spoken of throughout the whole world. (Rom. 1:8)

[I]f indeed you continue in the faith, grounded and steadfast, and are not moved away from the hope of the gospel which you heard, which was preached to every creature under heaven, of which I, Paul, became a minister. (Col. 1:23)

Third, we have to deal with our curiosity about the "abomination of desolation."† This abomination had already occurred once, under the tyranny of Antiochus Epiphanes. Jesus says it will happen again in the holy place (v. 15), and it would affect everyone in Judea (v. 16). This probably refers to the desecration of the temple which occurred under the Jewish rebels against Rome, although some apply it to the Romans themselves.

† the **"abomination of desolation"**: *a monumental act of desecration. Historically, this phrase often refers to the actions of Antiochus Epiphanes, who profaned the Jewish Temple by having a pig sacrificed upon its altar.*

Then there is the matter of the "clouds of heaven." In verse 30, we see the sign of the Son of man, who is in heaven. This is His judicial act against Jerusalem, and He sends out His messengers all over the Gentile world (v. 31). Remember to consider Daniel 7:13. The one like the Son of Man comes on the clouds of heaven into the heavenly courts. This is not a coming down to earth. It is not referring to what we call the Second Coming, but rather to the Ascension. This is the first formal act of Christ's rule, established in the Ascension ten years previous.

We must also learn the lesson of the fig tree, not neglecting to notice that the fig tree lesson was an enacted parable about the destruction of the Temple. Within one generation, Jesus says that these signs will bud, and the summer (not *winter*) will be near. He reinforces His words with a strong word—heaven and earth might fold, but His words, never. And everything He said did come to pass within the course of *one* generation. Far from being an embarrassingly false prediction, this chapter is one of the great means of authenticating Christ as a true prophet of God. Of course, He was much more than this, and so we must bow down and worship Him.

† **Luke 17:35–37:** *Two women shall be grinding together; the one shall be taken, and the other left. Two men shall be in the field; the one shall be taken, and the other left. And they answered and said unto him, Where, Lord? And he said unto them, Wheresoever the body is, thither will the eagles be gathered together.*

† **Matthew 24:36–41:** *But of that day and hour knoweth no man, no, not the angels of heaven, but my Father only. But as the days of Noe were, so shall the coming of the Son of man be. For as in the days that were before the flood they were eating and drinking, marrying and giving in marriage, until the day that Noe entered into the ark,* and knew not until the flood come and took them away; *so shall the coming of the Son of man be. Then shall two be in the field; the one shall be taken, and the other left. Two women shall be grinding at the mill; the one shall be taken, and the other left.*

And last, "I wish we'd all been ready." What is the meaning of "one is taken and the other left"? This is commonly thought to refer to the rapture—one taken up into heaven, and the other left on earth to kick himself for not praying the sinner's prayer when he had a chance. On the bright side, there will be a lot of free, unmanned cars available. But compare Luke 17:35–37† with the parallel passage, Matthew 24:36–51.† The one who is taken is taken off to judgment, just like those judged by God in the day of Noah. The one who is left is *spared*. This is not about the rapture at all.

As shown at the beginning of the chapter, it is important to realize that the disciples are not asking a series of disconnected questions. Their questions hang together, and we must not try to cram several thousand years in between the answers. In Matthew 24:4–13, Jesus warns His disciples to be on guard against false signs of the end before the end. There was going to be a great deal of turmoil *in the Roman Empire* prior to the destruction of Jerusalem (not all of it connected to Israel), and Jesus did not want them to panic at every new crisis. He then comes to the point of their question—the end of the age, *not* the end of the cosmos.

But what about some things in this chapter that *obviously* couldn't have happened in the first century?

Immediately after the tribulation of those days the sun will be darkened, and the moon will not give its light; the stars will fall from heaven, and the powers of the heavens will be shaken. Then the sign of the Son of Man will appear in heaven, and then all the tribes of the earth will mourn, and they will see the Son of Man coming on the clouds of heaven with power and great glory. And He will send His angels with a great sound of a trumpet, and they will gather together His elect from the four winds, from one end of heaven to the other. (Mt. 24:29–31)

This is the passage that confuses many. How could these events be speaking of the first century? The answer is found in the Old Testament passages that Jesus is quoting. We saw in the last chapter that we are to let the New Testament writers instruct us on what Old Testament passages mean. This is an instance where the enlightenment flows the other way—from the Old to the New.

At first glance it *does* look like the end of the world, but the verse is a quotation from Isaiah 13:10 and 34:4. How is it used *there?* In the original passages, the imagery referred to the destruction of Babylon (13:1) and it meant the same thing for Edom (34:5). We should therefore assume that Jesus is talking about the same kind of thing when He quotes those passages. He is prophesying the destruction of Jerusalem in A.D. 70. He is saying to Jerusalem, "*Your* lights are going to go out. *Your* sun is going down."

Someone might argue that Jesus was quoting Isaiah but using his words to a very different purpose. This is not likely. Everywhere there is similar "collapsing solar system" imagery in the Old Testament (see Ezek. 32:7; Amos 8:9; Joel 2:28–32), the reference is always to the same thing—the destruction of nations and cities. There is no scriptural reason to handle such passages differently when they are quoted in the New Testament, *especially* when they are quoted in response to a question about when Jerusalem was going to be destroyed. Everywhere the Bible uses this kind of language, it is applied to the judgment of God falling on a particular nation or city—Babylon, Edom, Egypt, the northern kingdom of Israel. There is no scriptural reason to think it is any different in Matthew 24.

In the aftermath of this cataclysmic judgment on Jerusalem, Christ's messengers (angels) are sent out to gather in the elect. This is referring to the great gospel work of proclaiming Christ's gospel throughout the entire earth.

And then, in the next few verses, Jesus teaches us a lesson from the fig tree.

> Now learn this parable from the fig tree: When its branch has already become tender and puts forth leaves, you know that summer is near. So you also, when you see all these things, know that it is near—at the doors! Assuredly, I say to you, this generation will by no means pass away till all these things take place. Heaven and earth will pass away, but My words will by no means pass away. (Mt. 24:32–35)

Christ teaches us here that all these events of the first century are signs of *summer*—not the long winter that historical pessimism assumes is characteristic of our age. Jesus also settles the matter of when *all these things* will happen: within one generation. The very generation of men which Jesus was teaching. And it *all* came to pass in A.D. 70, just as He said. He was a great prophet indeed.

Questions for Discussion
When biblical prophets begin speaking in a way that is unlike what we are used to, one of the things we must do is turn to the Bible for direction on how to interpret that kind of language.

1. What does language describing a "collapsing solar system" mean in the Old Testament? Does taking it this way in the New Testament fit the context?
2. When the Son of Man came on the clouds of heaven, where did He come?
3. If we take Matthew 24 as applying to the destruction of Jerusalem in A.D. 70 what impact does this have on our views of Christ as a prophet.

13.

666 AND ALL THAT

Leftover Bits from the Old Way of Thinking, Part 2

The gloomy old reprobate Ambrose Bierce said this about the book of Revelation: "A famous book in which St. John the Divine concealed all that he knew. The revealing is done by the commentators, who know nothing."* It is indeed unfortunate that we by our sloth have made a *revelation* into one of the most obscure books of the Bible.

As we seek to understand Revelation, the question will arise— "Do you take this book literally?" Well, we are Christians, and this means we *believe* the book. But if the questioner means "Is this book a blow-by-blow account of the exact manner that these events will unfold?", the answer is that we take *parts* of it literally, which means that other portions cannot be taken that way. Most contemporary Christians reverse the order, but everyone takes some parts literally and other portions symbolically.

Here are some guidelines. The position argued here holds that the book of Revelation, with the exception of the last three chapters, was fulfilled two thousand years ago. This means, incidentally, that we take the date of the writing of Revelation to be prior to A.D. 70.

---

*Ambrose Bierce, *The Devil's Dictionary* (New York: Dover Publications, 1958), 113.

The two choices are an early date (pre-A.D. 70) and a late date (post-A.D. 70, probably in the 90s). There are many fine scholars who hold to both positions. The evidence for a late date is generally external to the book itself—i.e., it largely depends upon on an ambiguous reference in the writing of the early church father Irenaeus.

The position held here is that Revelation was written prior to A.D. 70 in large part because we take certain clear statements in the book at face value. We can date the book *internally*. First, this is what the book *directly* says:

> The Revelation of Jesus Christ, which God gave Him to show His servants—*things which must shortly take place.* (Rev. 1:1; cf. 1:3, 19; 22:6–7, 12, 20)

In either case, whether it was written early or late, Revelation teaches that its predicted events were to come to pass shortly thereafter. So this means that Revelation is not talking about the end of the world.

Secondly, this is what the book *indirectly* says. In Daniel 8:26, the prophet is told to seal up his prophecy because it is a long way off. The event proved it to be about four hundred years away. But John hears this: "And he said to me, 'Do *not* seal the words of the prophecy of this book, *for the time is at hand*'" (Rev. 22:10). What does this mean for us two thousand years later? It seems likely that Daniel and John are talking about the same thing.

And third, this enables us to make sense of the prophecies in a way which fits them "literally" and also dates the book. History happened in a certain way, but for the creative, the future is infinitely malleable.

Fourth, this means that the book was not meaningless to its original recipients, the seven churches of Asia. John says to his *first* readers, "Let him who has understanding . . . " (Rev. 13:18).

One of the reasons we're so confused about the book of Revelation is that we have drifted away from the classical education of earlier times. This type of education provided, in some *small* measure, the kind of information which the residents of these cities had from their "newspapers." Nero was an animalistic pervert. He kicked one of his pregnant wives to death. He murdered his mother. He set Christians on fire to serve as lamps for a dinner party. He would dress up as a beast and rape both male and female prisoners. And he was the covenant head of Rome—that great Satan.

He had the number of a man. Latin, Greek, and Hebrew all used letters for numerals. We use Roman letters and Arabic numerals, but they used their letters for both purposes. In Hebrew, using *their* numbering system, the name *Neron Kesar* adds up to 666. There is no need to "massage" the numbers. And if you take it in another spelling and in Latin, as an ancient scribe mistakenly might, you get 616, one of the textual variants of the number in our manuscripts.

John also points to the line of emperors. The beast was the Roman Empire, a city seated on seven hills. But the seven heads of the beast had another signification. "There are also seven kings. Five have fallen, one is, and the other has not yet come" (Rev. 17:9–10). The first five Caesars were Julius, Augustus, Tiberius, Caligula, and Claudius. The sixth Caesar was Nero, who was reigning when Revelation was written. Five have fallen, and one *is*.

Then there is the question of the forty-two months: "And he was given a mouth speaking great things and blasphemies, and he was given authority to continue for forty-two months" (Rev. 13:5–7). Nero was the first Roman emperor to persecute the saints, and he did so from November 64 to June 68 . . . forty-two months.

Nero was *the* blasphemer. Asia was the center of emperor worship, and it was where our seven churches were located. Nero most certainly received "great things and blasphemies." He had an immense statue of himself in his palace, and received accolades such as "The Eternal One! Thou august! Sacred voice!" Nero was one of the great blasphemers of history.

We have many other reasons to identify Nero as a principal figure in this book. He was the head of the beast which is the focus of the wrath of our Lord Jesus Christ, the ruler of the kings of the earth.

We also see that Nero provides us with a case study of what the Lord Jesus does when He wields the rod of iron. Rebellion against heaven is judged. Because of such judgments, we are told that the kings of the earth will (eventually) bring their honor and glory into the New Jerusalem (Rev. 21:24). But why would they see it in this way when *we* do not see it in this way? How can we preach to kings when we don't believe what they are commanded to believe?

A lot of these things seem strange to us, but only because we are unfamiliar with the historical events of the first century. Once we are familiar with what happened back then, it becomes a very plausible time for the fulfillment of these prophecies.

The first emperor of Rome was *Julius Caesar.* Although he never took the title emperor on account of the anti-monarchical prejudice of the Romans, he was an emperor in fact, and he was reckoned as such. He reigned from 49–44 B.C. Following him was *Caesar Augustus.* Christ was born during the reign of Augustus. Although he was a decent leader on the political level, he allowed himself to be worshiped as deity. The cult of emperor worship was begun under his reign and was particularly strong in Asia Minor. The seven churches of the early chapters of Revelation were located in Asia Minor. Augustus reigned from 27 B.C. to A.D. 14. His reign was considered the golden age of the Roman Empire. After Augustus, the moral character of the emperors plunged drastically.

Next was *Tiberius Caesar,* who reigned from A.D. 14–37 and under whose reign Jesus was crucified. After that was *Gaius Caesar,* more popularly known as *Caligula.* He reigned from A.D. 37–41. It is important to notice that Caligula was reigning during the formative years of the Christian church. He was also the instigator of an incident which may have been referred to in the New Testament. He ordered a statue of himself to be set up in the Temple at Jerusalem and sent a man named Petronius with an army to enforce the edict. Only Caligula's death prevented a war at that time. The hunger for worship, for divine honors, was very evident, and it was not hard for the early Christians to see the formation of the beast in the hubris of their emperors.

Then came *Claudius.* He reigned from A.D.. 41–54. Next was the most infamous of them all, *Nero Caesar.* His reign was from A.D. 54–68. He killed himself in the summer of 68, leading to a tumultuous year, which can be called "The Year of the Four Emperors." The death of Nero resulted in civil war. He was followed by *Galba,* who managed to hang onto the throne for only seven months. Galba was replaced by *Otho,* who in turn was replaced by *Vitellius.* Vitellius was replaced by the general *Vespasian* who had been conducting the war in Judea, which was not yet over. Vespasian left his son *Titus* in charge of the remainder of the war. Vespasian restored order, became emperor, and his son became emperor after him.

The formation of the Church overlaps with these events. Christ was born around 4 B.C., and His ministry ended in the mid to late A.D. 20s. The church was greatly expanded shortly after, following the gift of the Spirit at Pentecost. The first book of the New Testament was probably Galatians, written in the early 40s. The rest of the New Testament was probably completed within the next thirty years. It makes the best sense of all the information we have to see that the entire canon of the New Testament was written before the destruction of the Temple in A.D. 70. Some books were written quite late, just a few years before this, like the book of Hebrews. But virtually all the books of the New Testament have an expectant air about them. They are all waiting for something drastic that will happen soon, and not one of them even *mentions* the most cataclysmic event in Jewish history—the fall of Jerusalem in A.D. 70—as being past. That event was the destruction of the old Judaic order and its replacement by the Christian church, the New Israel.

The Old Testament and the New Testament make us expect a significant event like this in A.D. 70 or thereabouts. The language of Revelation is full of Old Testament language and allusions, all of which make us look for an event that includes the destruction of the Temple and the judgment of Israel, as well as big changes on the world stage of politics. And sure enough, we can confirm that the political changes did indeed take place and that John was fairly blatantly pointing at particular emperors.

In other words, we must remember that if we were permitted to read all the "newspapers" of that era, it would throw a completely different light on the contents of the New Testament. And while we do not have all that information, we do have much more than we usually pay attention to. It is a very well documented era in history. It is important to look for the intention of any New Testament writer with regard to the understanding of *his first readers.*

The Jewish revolt, when it came, was utterly crushed. But at the time it began, the revolt looked to be quite promising. Nero died in A.D. 68. The revolt began around the same time (67–68) and did not end until three years later when Titus took the city of Jerusalem in A.D. 70. Remember that during this same time, Rome was involved in her own civil wars and struggles for the throne, and the barbarians on the northern frontier were restless. It was a time of great turmoil and civil uncertainty *for the Romans*. Nevertheless, the war ended in A.D. 70 with the utter destruction of the Jewish state, just as Jesus had predicted. The Jews had been the principal persecutors of the Christians and this hindrance was now gone—although the Romans quickly replaced them. At first, the great whore of Babylon rode the beast. Afterwards the beast continued persecuting the church by itself.

Questions for Discussion

When we read the Bible, we have to assume a certain amount of "background knowledge," the kind of knowledge you might get from newspapers or history books. And when we read certain passages, we have to ask whether the newspapers of the first century or the newspapers of the twenty-first century fill out the context better.

1. Does this approach to the book of Revelation take the book "literally"?
2. What are some of the basic reasons for an early date for the book of Revelation?
3. Who were the emperors of Rome that corresponded to John's "seven heads"?

14.

THE NEW HUMANITY

West to Eden

Genesis is the book of beginning. This is too often neglected by Christians. Here we see the beginning of the world, obviously, but also the beginning of marriage, of work, of rest, of music, and of many other of God's good gifts. In short, the book of Genesis provides us with a basic understanding of our relationship to the world around us. What are we supposed to *do* while we are here?

> Then God blessed them, and God said to them, "Be fruitful and multiply; fill the earth and subdue it; have dominion over the fish of the sea, over the birds of the air, and over every living thing that moves on the earth." (Gen. 1:28)

> So God blessed Noah and his sons, and said to them: "Be fruitful and multiply, and fill the earth. And the fear of you and the dread of you shall be on every beast of the earth, on every bird of the air, on all that move on the earth, and on all the fish of the sea. They are given into your hand. Every moving thing that lives shall be food for you. I have given you all things, even as the green herbs." (Gen. 9:1–3)

So here are our marching orders. This command from God has historically been called *the cultural mandate*. Before the Fall, God expressly gave dominion to mankind over all creation. This is seen in the passage from the first chapter of Genesis. But God reiterates this charge to Noah. Noah lived after the Fall, and this mandate is given immediately after a stupendous judgment on sin. The presence of sin obviously does not lift or remove the cultural mandate.

In radical environmental circles, the current dogma is that man is the cancer of the planet. Under girding many of the political controversies of our day is an unbiblical view of reality which assumes that everything in the world is on an equal footing, with the odd exception of man. This is what drives contemporary environmentalism. At the same time, environmental extremists cannot help but reveal a faint acknowledgment of the existence of this cultural mandate because *we* are somehow responsible to fix everything. But in the Christian view the problem is not pollution, but rather sin. We must take care not to simply react to contemporary extremists, animal rights nuts, etc. Our position is to be the *biblical* one, and not a reactionary one. Consider the following, for just a couple examples:

> Woe to those who join house to house; they add field to field, till there is no place where they may dwell alone in the midst of the land! (Is. 5:8)

> A righteous man regards the life of his animal, but the tender mercies of the wicked are cruel. (Prov. 12:10)

Isaiah makes it clear that Christians should not be out to "pave the planet." And in Proverbs Solomon makes it plain that believers should treat animals with decency and respect. These duties are to be defined by Scripture, and not by environmental extremists, but they *are* duties nonetheless. So the problem is sin, not the existence of *man* as such. The Bible teaches that creation is *fallen* and groans as in the pains of childbirth (Rom 8). This is the result of sin, it is not sin itself. The Bible always defines sin in terms of disobedience to God's law. Sin is not found in the material world or in a *part* of the material world (i.e., the presence of mankind).

The cultural mandate is nothing more or less than mankind's obligation to be culturally responsible. That responsibility is to be defined by what God says in Scripture, and not by the latest jag that secularist unbelievers might be on. Words like "responsibility" are not neutral, and we must always be grounded in Scripture. And so this cultural responsibility must always have the gospel at the center of it, and various details of cultural application as the overflow.

Consider Psalm 8, which includes a promise of restoration of all things in Christ. The author of the book of Hebrews takes this passage from the Psalms and plainly applies it to *mankind in Christ.* Consider his application of the psalm. The mandate remains in force for impotent man, but this simply means that we do not have the power to do rightly what God requires us to do. But part of the good news is that this impotence has been finally removed in Christ.

> For He has not put the world to come, of which we speak, in subjection to angels. But one testified in a certain place, saying: "What is man that You are mindful of him, or the son of man that You take care of him? You have made him a little lower than the angels; You have crowned him with glory and honor, and set him over the works of Your hands. You have put all things in subjection under his feet." For in that He put all in subjection under him, He left nothing that is not put under him. *But now we do not yet see all things put under him.* But we see Jesus, who was made a little lower than the angels, for the suffering of death crowned with glory and honor, that He, by the grace of God, might taste death for everyone. For it was fitting for Him, for whom are all things and by whom are all things, in bringing many sons to glory, to make the captain of their salvation perfect through sufferings. (Heb. 2:5–10)

To this, there are three possible responses. One is like the man who buried his talent in the ground because he feared a harsh master. Cultural responsibility to exercise dominion in the world is just too difficult and hard, and so an *escapist religion* is born. A second man likes the idea of "dominion" and so he begins to eat and drink and beat the fellow servants, resulting in a *despotic religion.* The third humbles himself and enters into godly dominion through and in Christ.

The Church continues to be hampered in the work of reformation by certain "unquestionable truths" that are still circulated among us. One of these "truths" is that the law of God amounts to slavery instead of freedom. But in the gospel, all things liberate us, including the law of God. Consider the preamble to the Ten Commandments, and notice how God is telling the people that His law is actually the law that liberates. This only makes sense in the context of the gospel of course, but we must insist that it *does* make sense in the context of the gospel.

> I am the LORD thy God, which have brought thee out of the land of Egypt, out of the house of bondage. (Exod. 20:2)

The Scriptures, from Genesis to Revelation, tell us the story of salvation, and they further tell us that salvation *is* a story. The salvation of God's people has never been a matter of disembodied truths for disembodied souls. And so it is that the Ten Commandments are not abstracted law but rather are introduced by God placing them in the right part of the story. The Ten Commandments begin with "once upon a time." God redeemed His people from Egypt, and in gratitude for this, and in light of this historical reality, they were solemnly covenanted to live in a certain grateful way. Grace is followed by gratitude, and gratitude knows no other response than obedience from the heart.

But false gods tell a false story. We live in a secular (anti-Christian) state, in a secular age, and both are eager to get rid of whatever remaining vestiges there may be of the older Christian order. How did this happen? False gods and false gospels have to function in the world that God made, and this means that they must operate within His categories, even as they attempt to distort and destroy those categories. This means they must also tell a story of "deliverance from Egypt."

†**the Reformation:** *the sixteenth-century revival of Christianity which sought to ground our beliefs in Scripture and denied that our good works are in any way responsible for our salvation. This revival was not well-received by the existing Roman church, which excommunicated and persecuted many of the Reformers. As a result, Protestantism was born.*

In our case, the story we've heard countless times concerns how the secular state, our supposed "savior," came to exist. As the story usually goes, after the Reformation,† Europe was torn apart with religious strife. The infamous "wars of religion" wracked Europe until finally, with a great sigh of relief, our fathers stumbled into the virtues of tolerance, and the secular state took over the public square. Our "deliverance" was that bloodthirsty religious convictions were finally banished into the realm of "personal belief"—a realm, of course, that had no effect on public behavior. In this story, not only are we saved by something other than the Christian gospel, but we are also saved *from* the Christian gospel. The story is compelling, widespread, constantly reiterated, and almost entirely false. Unfortunately, even many Christians have been taken in by aspects of it. This is how most Christians in the West have made their peace with the "escapist" option mentioned earlier. Religion is to have no effect on our views of what should and should not be allowed in the public square, but may be allowed to inform us what will get us salvation in the next life.

The Church has been relegated to a position of lesser importance, even in the United States where professing Christians constitute a large segment of the population. In large measure, this is because many Christians believe the secular story they were told. In the back of their minds, they are worried about the cultural pandemonium that would be brought about if Christians gain undue influence. Outlaw abortion and what is next? Obviously bloodshed between Lutheran states and Catholic states, just like in the old days. The story has done its work on us.

Christians, therefore, tend to divide into two major categories. The first are contented inhabitants of the evangelical ghetto. They want to escape from all public responsibilities, and they conceive the faith as something that will enable us to escape from this evil world. The secular state is *wrong* but unconquerable. Satan is the god of this world, and what we need to do is pray for the rapture to whisk us all out of here—as though, as mentioned earlier, God's work in this world was like America's disastrous involvement in Vietnam, and the end of the world simply a cosmic version of the evacuation of Saigon. Some views think this will be done *en masse,* all at once near the end of the world. Others believe that God evacuates us one at a time as we die—this is the "Jesus, take me home" option. But the point of everything is to make it to heaven when you die.

The second group wants a place at the table. They do not like being marginalized, with their voice *completely* unheard, and they want to be invited to the discussions. They accept the idea of the secular state and the democratic ethos that goes with it, but simply want their voice to be registered along with all the others. The secular state is *right* but is currently not living up to its promising potential because the Christians are inexplicably excluded. As the babble of special interest voices ascends up to the secular throne, these Christians want to make sure that a representative evangelical voice is numbered among them.

But Christian worship is the declaration that God is creating a new humanity in Christ, and wherever that new humanity gathers, a new center is constituted, a new public square is established. We reject the ghetto-izing of the faith, which wants to worship God without actually creating a city. The only way to accomplish this is by distorting what the Scriptures actually say. Treasure the text, but do it in a way that pulls the punch.

So we also reject the idea that Christ can be considered "a player." He is no player; He is the Lord of heaven and earth. How is this to be accomplished? The answer that the Bible gives, from beginning to end, is that such things are always done by faith. The power of the Holy Spirit operates when the Word of God is declared in faith. "For whatsoever is born of God overcometh the world: and this is the victory that overcometh the world, *even our faith*" (1 Jn. 5:4). How are we to subdue kingdoms? By faith, as we are told in Hebrews (11:33). How are we to bring every thought captive (2 Cor. 10:3–6)? Not by carnal means but by faith.

The Christian church is far more than mother of the faithful. She is called to be mother of cities. And where shall the root of these new cities be planted? Wherever the Word and the sacrament are. If God grants a genuine reformation, it will be one like that which was granted in the sixteenth century, and the most obvious common feature it will share with that earlier reformation will be that it *challenges* the rulers of this age. No greater indictment of the contemporary church than this can be found: the secular state is operating on all cylinders, and yet for the most part, the Christian pulpit remains a *safe* place to be.

More pastors ought to wonder about this. Shouldn't ministers and churches be more concerned than they are about the lack of opposition they are facing? And shouldn't they be willing to consider if it isn't the result of diluting the message. It is possible to talk about the final judgment and the lordship of Jesus Christ in such a way that makes it clear that He is only lord over those areas that secularists are frankly happy to let Him have—the afterlife, for example. Who cares if Jesus is Lord in ways that never make any difference at all?

This is not the way it should be. The worship of the Christian church is the New Jerusalem, descending down out of heaven. As churches are built and faithful worship is established, as converts are baptized and taught, as parents raise their children in the nurture and admonition of the Lord, as the nations are brought into the faith, they are being incorporated into the New Jerusalem, the city of the new humanity.

> Ye also, as lively stones, are built up a spiritual house, an holy priesthood, to offer up spiritual sacrifices, acceptable to God by Jesus Christ. Wherefore also it is contained in the scripture, Behold, I lay in Sion a chief corner stone, elect, precious: and he that believeth on him shall not be confounded. (1 Pet. 2:5–6)

The Christian faith is not "a belief system"; it is the future of the human race. In Jesus Christ, God has reconstituted our humanity, and we are growing up into Him as God is restoring the image of God in us. That image was defaced (not annihilated) in the rebellion of Adam, but God has created an opportunity for us to come back into a complete and restored humanity again—in Christ. Not only has He remade us this way, but He has also given us a place to live. That place is the New Jerusalem.

The New Jerusalem is quite clearly a symbol for the Christian church, provided we read certain passages together. This is a glorious symbol which exists even outside the book of Revelation. Consider:

But he who was of the bondwoman was born according to the flesh, and he of the freewoman through promise, which things are symbolic. For these are the two covenants: the one from Mount Sinai which gives birth to bondage, which is Hagar—for this Hagar is Mount Sinai in Arabia, and corresponds to Jerusalem which now is, and is in bondage with her children—but the Jerusalem above is free, which is the mother of us all. For it is written: "Rejoice, O barren, You who do not bear! Break forth and shout, You who are not in labor! For the desolate has many more children Than she who has a husband." (Gal. 4:23–27)

The same thing is taught in Hebrews.

But you have come to Mount Zion and to the city of the living God, the heavenly Jerusalem, to an innumerable company of angels, to the general assembly and church of the firstborn who are registered in heaven, to God the Judge of all, to the spirits of just men made perfect, to Jesus the Mediator of the new covenant, and to the blood of sprinkling that speaks better things than that of Abel. (Heb. 12:22–24)

This helps us to understand the symbolism in the last pages of the Bible, the symbolism of a welcoming invitation. The old humanity is summoned to become the new humanity in Christ.

Then one of the seven angels who had the seven bowls filled with the seven last plagues came to me and talked with me, saying, "Come, I will show you the bride, the Lamb's wife." And he carried me away in the Spirit to a great and high mountain, and showed me the great city, the holy Jerusalem, descending out of heaven from God. (Rev. 21:9–10)

The Jerusalem above is the mother of all who believe. We who believe have come to a Mount Zion that cannot be touched, that is, we have come to the heavenly Jerusalem. And when the angel showed John the great city, the holy Jerusalem coming down out of heaven from God, he was being shown the bride of Christ. The Christian church is therefore the bride of Christ, the wife of the Lamb. The Christian church is the New Jerusalem. All Christians are living stones in this great City and Temple (1 Pet. 2:4). The Christian church is advancing through the world, like a bride coming down the aisle in her glory.

Questions for Discussion

Although the Bible is a collection of sixty-six books, it is important for us to recognize that there is one guiding Author throughout, and this means that we have to learn how to read from Genesis to Revelation seeing the same central themes.

1. What is the cultural mandate? How does this relate to a modern Christian's obligations with regard to cultural responsibility?
2. What are the three basic kinds of religion?
3. What are the arguments for identifying the New Jerusalem with the Christian Church?

15.

COMPLETELY NUTS

Faith is Exegetically Indefensible

We sometimes assume that sound exegesis of the Scriptures is a scientific operation, one in which a believer or an unbeliever—provided they know "the rules"—can come away with a right understanding of what the Bible is saying. Of course, there is an element of truth in this—grammatical and lexical meanings can be objective enough. But with that said, we have to acknowledge that the central vision presented in Scripture is something that only genuine faith can see.

What is the right intersection between Scripture and the world, and what is the role that faith is to play in understanding this rightly? Suppose a precocious young boy, after his father has finished saying grace over the evening meal, asked something like this. "Dad, how do we *know* that God gave us this food for *blessing?* Couldn't He just be fattening us up for the day of slaughter?" The father's answer is simple: "We know because the Bible said so." The father can say this even though his family's last name is not in the concordance, and cannot be found in Scripture anywhere.

> So then faith cometh by hearing, and hearing by the word of
> God. (Rom. 10:17)

> Now faith is the substance of things hoped for, the evidence of
> things not seen. (Heb. 11:1)

Faith is the natural response to the perceived faithfulness of God.
And the faithfulness of God is seen preeminently in His *promises.*
"Through faith also Sara herself received strength to conceive seed,
and was delivered of a child when she was past age, *because she judged
him faithful who had promised*" (Heb. 11:11).

Scripture tells us that a man reaps what he sows (Gal. 6:7). The
Bible tells us that all who desire to live a godly life in Christ Jesus
will be persecuted (2 Tim. 3:12). This presents us with an interpre-
tive problem. Manasseh was thrown into chains so that he might
repent (2 Chr. 33:11–12). Paul was thrown into chains in order to
rejoice and sing hymns to God (Acts 16:25). This is a hermeneutical
issue, but *what* are we interpreting? Faith must interpret the text *in
order* to interpret the world. We do not interpret the text *instead* of
interpreting the world.

We have to be careful not to fall into an *either/or* hole here.
You have a cousin in Oklahoma who, with regard to Cadillacs and
Lear jets, is busy "naming and claiming" every gaudy thing he can
think of. And you have another cousin in Grand Rapids, this one
a historical pessimist, who is living out his remaining days in the
gathering gloom.

But consider what different kinds of things faith accomplishes.
The *italics* mark a distinct change in tone.

> And what shall I more say? for the time would fail me to tell
> of Gedeon, and of Barak, and of Samson, and of Jephthae; of
> David also, and Samuel, and of the prophets: who through faith
> subdued kingdoms, wrought righteousness, obtained promises,
> stopped the mouths of lions, quenched the violence of fire, es-
> caped the edge of the sword, out of weakness were made strong,
> waxed valiant in fight, turned to flight the armies of the aliens.
> Women received their dead raised to life again: *and others were
> tortured, not accepting deliverance; that they might obtain a better
> resurrection: and others had trial of cruel mockings and scourg-
> ings, yea, moreover of bonds and imprisonment: they were stoned,
> they were sawn asunder, were tempted, were slain with the sword:*

they wandered about in sheepskins and goatskins; being destitute, afflicted, tormented; (of whom the world was not worthy:) they wandered in deserts, and in mountains, and in dens and caves of the earth. And these all, having obtained a good report through faith, received not the promise: God having provided some better thing for us, that they without us should not be made perfect. (Heb. 11:32–40)

Let's consider three examples of promises. Consider first the promise of salvation (Rom. 10:9–10). But not all faith is genuine (Jas. 2:19), and no Bible verse names any one of us specifically. And what of the promise of answered prayer (Jn. 16:23)? The Bible also teaches us that not all requests are in the will of God (Jas. 4:3). And there is the promise that our children will be faithful (Ps. 103:17). But then, what are we to make of Esau and Samuel's sons, and the many instances of covenantal unfaithfulness that we have personally seen?

What this means is that whenever *you* are trusting God for something He has promised, you can always be (and probably will be) challenged by means of arguments from the Bible. That is because faith cannot be forced out of the text in such a way as to compel unbelief to see it. But such challenges are really unbelief masquerading as a high view of the text. One of the central realities of Scripture, to which we must return, is that faith overcomes the *world* (1 Jn. 5:4).

Questions for Discussion

Returning to the beginning of the book, when Abraham saw what he did, he would not have been able to prove his position to an "objective" bystander. God spoke and Abraham believed. And as George MacDonald put it, "Obedience is the great opener of eyes."

1. Is "objective" exegesis—such that faith and unbelief are irrelevant—really possible? Why or why not?
2. Does faith in God's promises require a "name it and claim it" approach?

3. If our names are not attached to them, how can we know that
   the scriptural promises really are for us? What are some of
   these promises?

EPILOGUE

Give the king your judgments, O God, and your righteousness to the king's Son. He will judge your people with righteousness, and your poor with justice. (Ps. 72:1–2)

As we conclude, a good thing to keep in mind is the need to constantly turn to fix our eyes on *Jesus,* the author and finisher of our faith. When we think through these issues carefully, we must recognize that the basic issue is really the view we maintain of Him.

Jesus Christ really is the Lord of *all* things in heaven and on earth. Consider what Paul tells us in Philippians 2:9–11. At the name of Jesus, every knee is to bow, and not just those in heaven. In heaven, and on earth, and under the earth, let Jesus Christ be praised. And so we are seeking nothing less than to exalt Him in every place.

Jesus Christ *is* Savior of the world. "And we have seen and testify that the Father has sent the Son as Savior of the world" (1 Jn. 4:14). Jesus did not come in order to *try* to save the world, if the uncooperative world would only let Him. He came to save the world; He will be satisfied with nothing less than a saved world. That was the whole point. Of course this must not be taken to mean that every last human being who ever lived will finally be saved. Our Lord's teaching on the terrible nature of everlasting fire excludes that option. So the fact that Christ will save the world does not mean that He will save every last individual who ever lived in it. But it does mean that He will save the world, and we need to take the word *world* in such a way that encompasses more than a tiny, huddled band of the elect, consisting of no more than thirteen or fourteen people. Every Bible believer must reject the universalism that denies the awful reality of the final judgment for unbelievers. But at the same time, God sent His Son to be the *Savior of the world.*

Jesus Christ is the Conqueror of the principalities and powers. "Now is the judgment of this world; now the ruler of this world will be cast out. And I, if I am lifted up from the earth, will draw all peoples to Myself. This He said, signifying by what death He would die" (Jn. 12:31–32). Before fallen man was brought to his majority, he was ruled by the principalities and powers and various other mediating agencies. God, by definition, has always been sovereign, but in the time of the Old Testament He was pleased to mediate that sovereignty through various celestial powers. But now God reigns through a reconstituted mankind, man in Christ.

God's work through Christ—the last Adam doing the aborted task abandoned by the first Adam—is the work that establishes the Kingdom of God. In one sense, God's sovereignty (His kingly authority) has always existed, by definition. God is always God. But the kingdom announced in the New Testament is a kingdom in which the fractured authority of man over all things is being restored. So the kingdom of God in the New Testament is not the point where God suddenly gains sovereignty. It is the point where man (in Christ) is graciously given a restored authority over the world.

Jesus Christ is the re-Creator of the heavens and earth. "Nevertheless we, according to His promise, look for a new heavens and a new earth in which righteousness dwells" (2 Pet. 3:13). The Father made the world through the Son, and the Father remade the world through the Son. This is why we observe the first day of the week . . . it is the day on which Christ rested after His work of *re*creation (Heb. 4:10).

Jesus Christ is King in the Kingdom of God.

> Then comes the end, when He delivers the kingdom to God
> the Father, when He puts an end to all rule and all authority
> and power. For He must reign till He has put all enemies under
> His feet. The last enemy that will be destroyed is death. (1 Cor.
> 15:24–26)

The Christian church is not a volunteer organization, where we may
come and go as we please. The Church of Christ is a monarchy, and
we are the subjects of the Lord Jesus.

Jesus Christ is also the great Prophet.

> For Moses truly said to the fathers, "The LORD your God will
> raise up for you a Prophet like me from your brethren. Him you
> shall hear in all things, whatever He says to you. And it shall be
> that every soul who will not hear that Prophet shall be utterly
> destroyed from among the people." (Acts 3:22–23)

Our views of the future must be formed by submission to the words
of Jesus Christ. This includes those words which tell us about the
nature of the kingdom and the fulfillment of the prophecies of old.
We should believe as we are told, even if the whole thing seems to
be too good to be true. Eye has not seen, or ear heard, what God has
prepared for those who love Him.

Jesus Christ is the Conqueror of the kings of earth.

> [A]nd from Jesus Christ, the faithful witness, the firstborn from
> the dead, and the ruler over the kings of the earth. To Him who
> loved us and washed us from our sins in His own blood, and has
> made us kings and priests to His God and Father, to Him be
> glory and dominion forever and ever. Amen. (Rev. 1:5–6)

In this, we must take care to avoid the corruptions of unbelieving
philosophical assumptions. Christ is not the Lord of some invisible
heavenly place; He is the Lord and Master of the town where you
live—and, of course, everywhere else. He purchased this world and
its inhabitants with His blood, and no impudent magistrate is going to successfully deny Him. He *will* have it. Fix it in your minds:
Christ rules *here.* But at the same time, His authority is extended by
spiritual means and not by political means. It has political results,

but His kingdom does not advance in the same way that other kingdoms do.

Jesus Christ is the Lord of the Church. "Now in the morning, as He returned to the city, He was hungry. And seeing a fig tree by the road, He came to it and found nothing on it but leaves, and said to it, 'Let no fruit grow on you ever again.' Immediately the fig tree withered away" (Mt. 21:18–19; 24:32). Our Lord is the master husbandman of His people. When branches must be cut, He cuts. When the tree must be nourished, He nourishes. He put away the majority of the Jews because of their unbelief. He warns us against similar follies, for He will do similar things. But not only does the Gardener remove branches, He also promises to restore them, the restoration of the Jews being the preeminent example.

And so our basic confession in these matters is this: *Jesus Christ is Lord.*

I began this short book by asking for a willing suspension of disbelief. What if the world were to be saved? What if the Great Commission were actually to succeed? What if the nations were to stream to Jesus Christ, believing in Him? How wonderful it would all be if all this could be true. The best part of the story is, it is.

A BRIEF GLOSSARY

Appendix A

In this brief book, I have tried to avoid "buzz words," and have simply talked about the concepts themselves. But there is an established vocabulary for many of these things, and if you would like to pursue this further, you will need a brief orientation in that vocabulary. And for those who already have an eschatological background, this might be helpful in sorting things out as well.

What is eschatology?

Eschatology is the study of the last days; a person's eschatology is his view of "the last days." The word is less frequently applied to the doctrine of heaven and hell.

The last days of what?

The answer to that question is what divides Christians into various schools of thought. For example, some think it refers to the last days of the world, while others believe the "last days" in the New Testament refers to the last days of the Judaic age, as well as to the last days of the world as we know it.

What does the word "hermeneutics" mean?

Hermeneutics refers to the art, science, and methodology of biblical interpretation. Obviously the way someone interprets the Bible will have an impact on the interpretation of the prophecies of the Bible. Thus the question of *hermeneutics* is very important in debates over eschatology.

What is a futurist?

A *futurist* is one who believes the prophecy of Revelation is yet to be fulfilled (that is, it is still future).

What is a historicist?

A *historicist* is one who believes the prophecy of Revelation was fulfilled and is being fulfilled down throughout all church history.

What is a preterist?

A *preterist* is one who believes that the prophecy of Revelation was largely fulfilled in the first century. The position held in this book is a *preterist* position.

What is an idealist?

An idealist is one who believes that the prophecy of Revelation is symbolic and applies to all human history in a non-literal way.

Are these schools of thought limited to Revelation?

No. The differences are seen most clearly there, but they generally apply to other prophecies of a similar nature, as might be found in Matthew 24 or Isaiah 52.

What is the millennium?

The *millennium* is a period of one thousand years of peace prophesied by the apostle John in Revelation 20. It is important to note that a number of interpreters do not take it as a literal one thousand trips around the sun. The millennium is a thousand years of peace that Christians enjoy fighting over.

How can I keep the different schools of thought straight in my mind? What do the various terms mean?
Using the word *millennium,* the easiest way to remember what the names mean is to concentrate on the prefix before the word *millennial.* That prefix tells when the return of Christ is anticipated with regard to the millennium. But it is important to remember that all the evangelical schools of thought listed below firmly hold to a belief in the *literal and physical* return of Christ at the end of history.

What is historic premillennialism?
Historic premillennialism is the view that Christ will return *prior* to the millennium, and that He will reign on earth during the millennium. The word *historic* is used because some of the early church fathers (like Justin Martyr) held this position.

What is dispensational premillennialism?
Dispensational premillennialism is a variant form of premillennialism which arose in the nineteenth century and is held by a large number of American evangelicals today. Many more Christians, who would not call themselves dispensationalists, have nevertheless picked up quite a few unique dispensational assumptions (as seen in their assumptions about Armageddon, the Beast, 666, the Antichrist, etc.). This view is that Christ will return prior to the millennium, but there are many additional aspects to this position besides what is found in historic premillennialism.

What is unique about dispensational premillennialism?
The distinctives of dispensationalism are numerous. Among others, one is that there will be a secret coming of Christ seven years before the millennium, and another that Christ will preside over a reestablished Jewish state during the millennium, Temple sacrifices and all.

What is amillennialism?
Amillennialism holds that there will not be a literal earthly millennium. The prefix therefore is one of negation. The amillennialist

does not believe there will be a literal millennium on earth. Rather, he interprets it in a spiritual sense, with glorified saints reigning with Christ in heaven. Thus we are in the millennium now, but in a spiritual sense.

What is postmillennialism?

Postmillennialism is the view that Christ will return at the *end* of the millennium. The millennium is generally understood as a golden age of gospel expansion, wherein the Great Commission is fulfilled. At the end of that period of time, when the nations have all been brought to the discipleship of Christ, He will return and destroy the last enemy, which is death. The position argued in this book has been a postmillennial position.

Most postmillennialists today hold that the millennium is in progress now, meaning that the millennium is not literally one thousand years. Some postmillennialists of the nineteenth century held that the millennium was literally one thousand years in length, and was the last one thousand years of the Church Age, which was must longer than a thousand years.

Can any of the terms above be combined?

Yes. Premillennialists of all kinds are futurists. They believe that the prophecies of the "end times" are largely unfulfilled. Postmillennialists and amillennialists can be either historicists or preterists. At the same time, most postmillennialists are preterists, and most amillennialists are idealists.

FOR FURTHER READING
Appendix B

Campbell, Roderick. *Israel and the New Covenant.* Tyler: Geneva Divinity School Press, 1980.

Chilton, David. *The Days of Vengeance.* Fort Worth: Dominion Press, 1987.

Chilton, David. *The Great Tribulation.* Fort Worth: Dominion Press, 1987.

Chilton, David. *Paradise Restored.* Tyler: Reconstruction Press, 1985.

Davis, John Jefferson. *The Victory of Christ's Kingdom.* Moscow: Canon Press, 1996. This is a very short introductory treatment of the subject. A quick read, and good for a fast orientation.

DeMar, Gary. *Last Days Madness.* Brentwood: Wolgemuth & Hyatt, 1991. In this book, DeMar does a good job in showing how much speculative craziness has affected our views of eschatology.

Gentry, Ken. *Before Jerusalem Fell.* Tyler: I.C.E., 1989. This book argues for an early date for Revelation—that is, that the book was written prior to the destruction of the Temple in A.D. 70. If the book had been written after that, then it would be difficult to make it a "prophecy" of what had already happened.

Gentry, Ken. *The Greatness of the Great Commission.* Tyler: I.C.E., 1990.

Gentry, Ken. *He Shall Have Dominion.* Tyler: I.C.E., 1992. This is the most thorough introductory treatment of the eschatological issues available.

Hardyman, Julian. *Glory Days.* Nottingham: InterVarsity Press, 2006.

Hegeman, David. *Plowing in Hope.* Moscow: Canon Press, 2007. A very fine introduction to a biblical and life-affirming approach to the cultural mandate.

Herman, Arthur. *The Idea of Decline in Western History.* New York: Free Press, 1997.

Kik, J. Marcellus. *An Eschatology of Victory.* Phillipsburg: P&R Publishing, 1991. This is a limited treatment of Revelation and the apocalyptic sections of Matthew.

Leithart, Peter. *Against Christianity.* Moscow: Canon Press, 2003. In this short book, Leithart shows how we have used various tricks and "isms" to spiritualize the kingdom right out of Christ's hands. Good thing it didn't work.

Mathison, Keith. *Postmillennialism.* Phillipsburg: P&R Publishing, 1999. This is the best introductory treatment of the basic eschatological issues available.

Symington, William. *Messiah the Prince.* Philadelphia: Christian Statesman Press, 1884. A good example of nineteenth-century postmillennial thought.

Wright, N. T. *Surprised by Hope.* San Francisco: HarperOne, 2008. Wright does not use any of the standard eschatological vocabulary, but his treatment of a number of the key passages is very helpful.

CPSIA information can be obtained at www.ICGtesting.com
Printed in the USA
LVOW06s1159170815

450403LV00015B/229/P